Shiloh

to

Vicksburg

Dear Eliza

An Eyewitness Account in the

Civil War Letters

of

Major Virgil H. Moats

e l w

ACKNOWLEDGEMENTS

The Civil War letters of Major Virgil H. Moats were collected from four members of the fourth and two members of the fifth generation. They are descendents of Virgil through Douglas (Dud) Moats and his son, Wright D. Moats. They are Barbara Baily and Phyllis Wagley of Adrian, Michigan; Vivian Leptrone of Clearwater, Florida; Kathryn (Sage) Walker of Pebble Beach, California; Robert D. Sage and William C. Sage of Seattle, Washington. Other material was contributed by Thomas C. Moats of Sherwood, Ohio and Vivian Mulholland of Brooklyn, Michigan.

The original letters have been contributed to the Clements Library of the University of Michigan, Ann Arbor, Michigan.

The historical material provided as a context of the letters has been drawn from:

The Encyclopaedia Britannica
  The Encyclopaedia Britannica Company, New York, 1910;

The Life of William Tecumseh Sherman
  O. O. Howard and W. F. Johnson, Edgewood Publishing Company, 1891; and

The Civil War
  Bruce Catton, American Heritage Publishing Company, New York, 1982.

SHILOH TO VICKSBURG
"Dear Eliza"

TABLE OF CONTENTS

LETTERS

ILLUSTRATIONS

MAPS

INTRODUCTION

The American Civil War was a human catastrophy of epic proportions. It left killing grounds in massive numbers, more than 2400, throughout the eastern and midwestern portions of the country, and over 600,000 young men were cut down in the prime of their lives. Only 25-30% of these deaths were the result of combat. The remainder died of disease because of the conditions under which the men lived and because of the primitive state of the art of medicine. Of the 220,000 Confederate soldiers who were taken prisoner, 26,436 (12%) died in prison. Of the 126,850 Federal soldiers who were captured during the war, 22,576 (15%) died in confinement.

In retrospect it seems clear that the final outcome was foreordained. The North had advantages near two to one in men, material, and most economic factors relevant to the waging of a war. It is doubtful if any conflict has been the subject of more written accounts than this American tragedy. Most of these are dry and impersonal.

The letters of Major Virgil H. Moats, the subject of this book, offer fragments of a very personal story. Virgil was a Union soldier. He participated in a great many military actions including three of the great battles in the west - Shiloh or Pittsburg Landing, the battle of Arkansas Post, and the assault on Vicksburg. He undertook to write a documentation of his experiences through letters to his wife, Eliza.

As you may well infer from those reproduced here, Virgil appears to have written a great many letters. Unfortunately, only a few have survived. It seems likely that some of them never reached Eliza and others may have been lost in a fire that destroyed Eliza's home in Defiance, Ohio in 1918, five years after her death in 1913. She was eighty years old and had been a widow for fifty years. It is fortunate, however, that among the surviving letters are eyewitness accounts of the battle of Shiloh or Pittsburg Landing, the operations at Arkansas Post, and much of the activity aimed at Vicksburg.

In addition to his letters to Eliza, two letters to his father survive and they are included in this volume. There are also two letters to Eliza from her brother Lay W. Richardson, and one letter addressed to 'Verge' from another of her brothers, John E. Richardson.

All of these letters dated from 1862 to 1864 are personal and graphic and convey a sense and feel of the people and their times.

The letters are the substance of this book. To make them somewhat more intelligible, I have made an effort to provide a minimum of the history of the Civil War with an emphasis on the campaigns in the west and especially those actions in which Major Moats was an active participant. Chronological charts have been printed relating the dates of the letters to significant dates in the war. Simple maps are also included to permit tracking of the movements of the soldier wh is our subject and author.

Edward L. Walker
Pebble Beach, California
June, 1984

Shiloh

to

Vicksburg

1861

VIRGIL

The will to war was rising.

Virgil Moats was busy with the normal late winter and spring chores on his farm in northern Ohio. It was early in 1861.

As plowing, planting, and harvesting proceeded that year among the farmers in Northern Ohio, the everyday affairs of family and community gradually faded in importance compared to the demands of the rapidly developing civil conflict, especially after the news of the First Battle of Bull Run in late July. The militia with their 90-day enlistments would no longer suffice. Sterner measures were required.

Virgil was an educated man. He had been a school teacher, justice of the peace and had served a term as sheriff. Now he was a thirty-three year old farmer on his own land, engaged in assembling larger holdings for his growing family. His second wife, twenty-eight year old Eliza, is the heroine of this story although we have none of her letters. Virgil had a son, then aged eleven

Eliza Richardson Moats

Virgil Henry Moats

who had survived a sister and a mother in a previous marriage. Eliza had given him two more sons, William then five, and Douglas about two. A daughter, Hattie, died that summer of 1861 at age three. Eliza was then pregnant with Virgil's fourth son, Charles.

As summer passed into fall with the harvest of his crops, Virgil came to feel he could no longer deny his duty to serve in the great cause. At age 20 he had served as a corporal in the cavalry in the Mexican war. His previous military experience and his obvious talents stood him in good stead. He enlisted on October 13th, 1861 and two days later was appointed as a 2nd Lieutenant. In less than a month he was made Captain.

Although the records are silent on the point, it is possible that the rapid promotions arose from his standing with the men of the unit. Early in the war it was common practice for the men to choose their officers through elections as they normally chose justices of the peace, sheriffs or officers in the local militia at home. While this custom often resulted in the election of men who were ignorant of military matters, who were able political vote-getters or men who were prominent in the community, Virgil, at least, had some military and organizational background.

EARLY DEVELOPMENTS OF THE CONFLICT

Barely a year before Virgil's enlistment, John Brown made his spectacular raid on Harper's Ferry and been hanged for his trouble. Lincoln had been elected in the previous November and inaugurated in March. By that time South Carolina, Mississippi, Florida, Alabama, Georgia and Louisiana had seceded from the Union. Virginia, North Carolina, Texas, Arkansas and Tennessee were soon to follow. Missouri, Kentucky and Maryland were divided, and many from these states fought on each side. There were many Southern sympathizers in the North and individuals who opposed secession in the South.

Fort Sumter in Charleston Harbor was bombarded by the Confederate forces under General Pierre G. T. Beauregard after the Union forces had refused to evacuate. The assault on Fort Sumter on April 13th marked the military beginning of the Civil War. The fall of the fort set off waves of emotion on both sides.

Washington was in a precarious position. Virginia and with it the Federal Navy yard at Norfolk and the arsenal at Harper's Ferry were controlled by the Rebels. At the time the Army consisted of only about 16,000 scattered Federal troops. Few of them were in the Washington area which was close to Richmond where there was a substantial and growing Confederate army. Lincoln called on the states for a levy of 75,000 militiamen who were to serve for ninety days. Most people in the North thought that the war would be over by the time their enlistments ran out. No one seemed to realize the eventual magnitude of the developing holocaust.

There were minor skirmishes, some involving civilians. Three days after the affair at Fort Sumter, thus on April 18, the Sixth Massachusetts Regiment on its way to Washington was attacked by a civilian mob in Baltimore with some casualties. When that state was reduced to order, the area became the front and later the base of the Northern armies. It was early May before men from New York and other Northern States arrived in sufficient numbers to ease the danger to the Northern capitol. Until troops could be spared to protect the railway through Maryland, all reinforcements for the national capitol had to be brought up to Annapolis by sea.

In the west, almost the whole year of 1861 was spent in preparations for the contest. Sea power in the north was growing during 1861, and the effort to blockade the South was increasingly effective during the year. On January 1, 1862, the North had 212 ships under commission. Among them were a number of gunboats built in the vicinity of Cairo, Illinois for use in campaigns along the waterways of the west.

There was minor action at St. Louis where Union forces spirited a cache of arms across the Mississippi for safety and then forced a pro-southern camp to surrender. When the captives were paraded through the streets of St. Louis, someone threw a stone and the Union soldiers started firing. More than 25 civilians were killed or fatally wounded.

A somewhat more military action was carried out by General George B. McClellan during June and July of 1861. McClelland was a West Point man who had distinguished himself during the Mexican War. With a group of Ohio and Indiana volunteers, he started out from Parkersburg on the Ohio River and moved east to capture a small force at Philippi. He then routed a larger Confederate group of 4500 men at Rich Mountain near Beverly. While these actions were minor, the reports of them were made to sound like major victories and helped to establish a very positive attitude toward McClellan among his men as well as with the authorities in Washington.

The first major battle of the war took place at Bull Run, 25 miles from Washington between July 18th and 21st, 1861. Both armies were enthusiastic but 'green.' Union forces under General Irvin McDowell, 35,000 strong, clashed with about 30,000 Rebels under Beauregard and General Joseph E. Johnston. The Federals were accompanied and followed by civilians from Washington who came along to see the show and have a picnic in the area while listening to the firing or even watching the combat.

There were major casualties on both sides before the Union forces began falling back. As they did so, the civilian baggage suddenly perceived their danger and began scurrying to get on the road back to Washington. When a few started running, the rout was on. Civilian and soldier alike tried to move east in panic, resulting in one of the largest traffic jams in history on the road to Fairfax and Washington. Fortunately for them, the Confederates were little better organized and either could not or would not follow up on their victory.

The party was over. The Federals had lost nearly 3000 men and the Confederates nearly 2000. There would be no more picnics at the battle sites, and there would be no more ninety-day-wonders, as the militiamen were called. The war was on in earnest. It was clear that it was going to last much longer and be bloodier than anyone had originally anticipated.

THE MAJOR THEATERS

Throughout the middle and critical period of the war two distinct campaigns were in progress. In the east, largely in Virginia, there were the great but indecisive campaigns fought largely within the 100 mile gap between the two hostile capitals, Richmond and Washington. In this theater it was primarily a war of attrition rather than one of capture and occupation of territory. Then as now, the bulk of public attention was devoted to this epic, bloody, seesaw struggle.

In the west the war was to be fought and won with Northern successes gradually cutting the South in twain in the valleys of the Ohio, the Cumberland, and the Tennessee and in the Mississippi basin.

12

CHRONOLOGY 1861

BIOGRAPHY   HISTORY

                          JAN.
                          *
                          FEB.
                          *
                          MAR.
                          * Lincoln Inaugurated
                          *
                          APR.
                          * Bombardment Fort
                          *   Sumter
                          *
                          MAY
                          *
                          JUNE
                          *
                          JULY
                          * First Battle of
                          *   Bull Run
                          AUG.
                          *
                          SEPT.
                          *
                          OCT.
Virgil Enlisted   *
Appointed 2nd Lt.   *
                          NOV.
                          *
                          DEC.
Appointed Captain   *

1862

VIRGIL

As Captain, Virgil helped organize the 48th Ohio Volunteer Infantry at Camp Dennison, not far from Cincinnati. This task was formally completed on the 17th of February, 1862. He was placed in command of Company F, made up primarily of men he had helped recruit in the vicinity of Defiance, Ohio. It included a brother, Homer, and a number of other relatives and neighbors.

A roster of Company F as it appears in an official History of Defiance County is included in a Postscript on the 48th Ohio Volunteer Infantry near the end of this book. A comparison of this roster with the text of some of Virgil's letters suggests that the official list is incomplete both in terms of personnel and the fate to which some of them came.

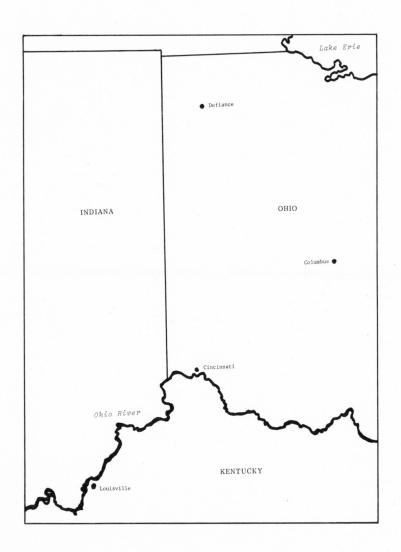

Lake Erie

● Defiance

INDIANA

OHIO

Columbus ●

● Cincinnati

Ohio River

KENTUCKY

● Louisville

Indiana, Ohio, Kentucky

18

Letter: Virgil to Eliza.

Feb. 11, 1862
Camp Dennison, Ohio

Dear Eliza

We arrived at Camp - or the boys rather - on Sunday night. We got to Columbus Saturday night one o'clock and learning that the 68th was going to start in the morning at 6, I sent the boys on and waited myself for the Reg. to go which did not get under way until noon Sunday. I found the boys and Boyd had next thing to the ague, but by evening he was about well. Whit was well. We came on down to Henid and there found the boys they having had to lie over and wait for us. Well we all got under way from the latter place and soon learned that the train would not stop at camp to let us off but would carry us to Cinti & then bring us back. So we all went to the city and transferred our stuff (15 boxes) on to the up train, and while I went to bid the boys goodbye, the train started & left me in the city all night. The boys all got back to camp that night. I got back Monday morning pretty well used up.

19

I found the boys well with 2 or 3 exceptions. Homer has gone to the city today to see Aunts folks. She is quite poorly. Homer is nearly over his cold.

Well we have just had our dinner. We cooked the rooster, got some flour & milk & made gravy and had a first class dinner, in fact I almost hurt myself eating, & still we have enough for supper left. John Richardson took dinner with us. Bill Roush has gone down to the city. I am Officer of Day this day and not in much of a humor for writing, therefore I will cut this letter short and write more next time. The 68th went to Paducah, Ky. Write soon as you get this and give me all the news.

Wal wrote to us not long ago.

Yours etc,
VHM

FACE-OFF IN THE WEST

General Henry Wager Halleck was in overall command of Union operations west of the Cumberland River. He was generally referred to as 'Old Brains' for his consummate skills of organization. Field command was in the hands of General Ulysses S. Grant. Under him were a number of Generals including W. T. Sherman, F. C. Smith, Lew Wallace, and John A. McClernand. Halleck had directed the building of a substantial fleet of river transport and gunboats at Cairo, Illinois. These were under command of Flag Officer A. H. Foote. East of the Cumberland and independent of Halleck, General Don Carlos Buell was in control.

Shortly after Virgil wrote the letter to Eliza from Camp Dennison, the 48th Ohio Volunteer Infantry departed to join Gen. Sherman, at Paducah, Kentucky. Sherman had been sent to Paducah to command the post about February 13th, 1862.

The Confederate forces opposing Halleck were under the overall command of General Albert Sidney Johnston. Among the Generals

21

under his command were Leonidas Polk and Pierre G. T. Beauregard.

At the beginning of 1862 the Confederate General Polk had followed a strategy of establishing a line passing through Bowling Green, Kentucky, Fort Donelson on the Cumberland, Fort Henry on the Tennessee and Columbus on the Mississippi. He was at Columbus where he had built forts and other works to command traffic on the Mississippi. General Beauregard had an army in western Tennessee and northern Mississippi.

MINOR WESTERN INCIDENTS

There were a number of small actions in the west but nothing of a decisive nature. A force under General James A. Garfield defeated a small Confederate force at Prestonburg in the mountains of eastern Kentucky. General G. H. Thomas won his first victory at Mills Springs or Logan's Cross Roads. General Johnston's army was forced to make a disasterous retreat in a battle on January 19-20.

In Missouri, in February, Captain Nathaniel Lyon, fearing that a stack of arms at the arsenal at St. Louis might fall into the hands of Confederate sympathizers, spirited most of the arms across the river to Illinois. He later (in May) captured a Confederate camp, paraded his prisoners through the streets of St. Louis, and incited a row in which 28 persons were killed.

General Samuel Curtis defeated General Earl Van Dorn in a battle at Pea Ridge, Arkansas on March 7-8. This victory essentially put an end to the war in that quarter.

THE UNION ASSAULT ON POLK'S LINE

Asked where to break the Confederate line stretching from Bowling Green to Columbus, General William T. Sherman said, "The center!" The center of Johnston's line was Fort Henry and Fort Donelson. Fort Henry was attacked by Grant and Flag Officer Andrew Foote on the 6th of February. The fort was poorly placed on low land, and the Tennessee River was at near flood stage. Foote's flotilla pounded it into submission before Grant could mount an attack with troops.

General Polk was replaced by General Johnston who had doubts about his ability to hold Polk's line under the attack of Grant, and he evacuated Bowling Green, sending 15,000 troops to Donelson and the remainder to Nashville.

Grant then moved overland to attack Donelson. After a battle which lasted for three days and in which the outcome was in doubt for some time, forces under Generals F. C. Smith, Lew Wallace, and John A. McClernand forced the surrender of the fort on the 16th of February, capturing 15,000 Confederates. It was at this point that Grant authored his often-quoted note, "No terms but immediate and unconditional surrender can be accepted."

The Tennessee River cut the center of the Southern line, and a continued campaign upstream (south) on the Tennessee was clearly the Union strategy. Johnston now no longer doubted but was convinced that he could not hold the northern line that had been established by Polk. He gave up Nashville and ordered General Beauregard to remove the garrison that was at Columbus and bring it to Corinth, Mississippi, a few miles south of Pittsburg Landing on the Tennessee.

On the Mississippi Union forces had seized New Madrid, but forces at Island 10 opposite New Madrid were a problem. A flotilla under Flag-Officer A. H. Foote was effective but a canal had to be cut to bring Union regiments to the rear. This was successfully accomplished on April 8, 1862 when the garrison of 7000 men surrendered.

VIRGIL

After a short rest at Paducah, Kentucky, Captain Virgil H. Moats and the 48th Ohio Volunteer Infantry moved with Sherman's army south. Their invasion of the South began as they traveled upstream on the Tennessee River aboard the steamer Express. They were a part of a force of 45,000 men.

Shiloh Church

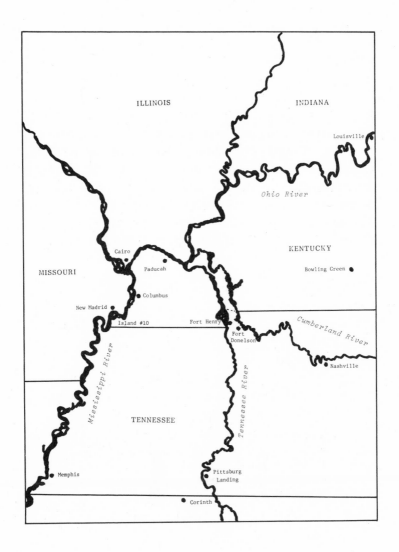

Route to Shiloh

CHRONOLOGY 1862
January to June

BIOGRAPHY   HISTORY

JAN.

VHM to Eliza   *

Camp Dennison   *

FEB.

* 48th Organized
*   Camp Dennison
* Fall of Fort Henry
* Fall of Fort
*   Donelson
* 48th Disembarks at
*   Pittsburg Landing
* Jefferson Davis
*   Inaugurated

MAR.

* Monitor Defeats
*   Merrimac

APR.

* Fall of Island #10
* Battle of Shiloh
*   Church

VHM to Eliza   * Capture of

Pittsburg Landing   *   New Orleans

MAY

* McClelland success
*   at Seven Pines

JUNE

* Lee Success at
*   Mechanicsburg

THE BATTLE OF SHILOH
OR PITTSBURG LANDING

The Battle of Shiloh or Pittsburg Landing has been called the second great battle of the American Civil War. It was fought on April 6th-7th, 1862 between the Union forces under General Grant and General Don Carlos Buell and the Confederates under General A. S. Johnston and General Beauregard. While Grant's army was traveling upstream on the Tennessee to Pittsburg Landing, the co-operating army under Buell was moving across country from Nashville to join Grant. Sherman was sent with General Stephen Augustus Hurlbut to occupy Pittsburg Landing, which he did on March 16. Virgil and the Ohio 48th were encamped near Shiloh Church, about two miles from the landing.

The Confederates had about 40,000 men at Corinth and they advanced on Pittsburg Landing with a view to beating Grant before Buell's forces could arrive. Their advance was delayed, unfortunately, by the wretched condition of the roads. Beauregard advised Johnston to give up the enterprise, but Johnston felt that a retreat would have a demoralizing effect on his raw troops, and he therefore resolved to continue his advance.

At 6 a.m. on the 6th of April, near Shiloh Church, the Confederate army advanced directly on the Landing. They quickly overran a brigade of the nearest Union division, that of Benjamin M. Prentiss, which had been sent forward from camp to reconnoiter.

The various Union divisions were dispersed in camps which were out of sight of one another. The Confederates spread around and between the local Federal camps as they encountered them. The two forward Union divisions were swiftly driven in on the others, who were given a little time to prepare themselves. The Union forces were certainly not prepared for battle and as a consequence did not immediately mount an organized response to the Confederate attack.

It was equally true that the Confederate commanders were unable to control and maneuver their troops. But the rear Union divisions, though alerted, were each in turn isolated and forced back, fighting hard, toward Pittsburg Landing. The remnant of Prentiss' division was cut off and forced to surrender. Another division lost its commander, General W. H. L. Wallace. On the Rebel side the disorder became greater and greater, many regiments were used up, and Johnston himself was killed in vainly attacking on a point of Wallace's line called the Hornet's Nest.

The day passed in confused and savage scuffles between the raw enthusiasts of either side, but by 5:00 p.m. Grant had formed a last and now a connected line of defense with Buell's leading division which had crossed the river, and all of his own infantry that he could rally. This line was hardly 600 yards from the Landing, but it was in a naturally strong position, and Beauregard suspended the attack at sunset. There was a last futile assault, delivered by some of the Confederate's brigades on the right that had not received Beauregard's order, against Buell's intact troops. They also came under the fire of the gunboats on the Tennessee. They were forced to retire.

During the night, Grant's detached division under Lew Wallace came up and the main body of Buell's group crossed the river. These together totaled more than 25,000 fresh troops. At 5 a.m. on the 7th, Grant took the offensive. Beauregard thereupon decided to extricate his sorely-tried troops from the misadventure and retired fighting toward Corinth. About Shiloh Church a strong rearguard under General Braxton Bragg repulsed the attacks of Grant and Buell for six hours before withdrawing, and all that Grant and Buell achieved was the reoccupation of the abandoned camps.

When the battle began there were 33,000 Federal troops, but Grant says there were no more than 25,000 in the line at any one time because so many ran in panic. The gunboats Tyler and Lexington were in effective position on the river. The Confederates had 40,000 the first day but no more than 20,000 in action on the second day. Wallace with his "Lost Division" arrived from Crumps Landing in the evening with 5,000 more, and Buell arrival with 20,000 to give the Union substantial numerical superiority on the second day.

Halleck was also accused of being remiss in allowing Buell's forces to march in a dilatory manner to join Grant, although Buell was not under Halleck's command. In any case, Buell's force arrived opposite the Landing, thus on the wrong side of the river, on the evening before the battle.

It was a Confederate failure but not a Union victory, and each side was seriously weakened. Neither made any movement in the next three weeks. The Union losses were over 13,000 killed, wounded and missing.

The Confederates official count was 10,700 lost, but it was probably more. As was often the case in this man-eating war, as many Confederate soldiers died of disease at Corinth in the next seven weeks as died in the combat itself.

There was great controversy at the time and it continues to this day concerning the quality of the generalship displayed by Grant and his superior, General Halleck. Grant had allowed his troops to set up camp without preparing defensive trenches and breastworks. Some of the troops were so green that some had never been shown how to load their muskets. Whether the lack of defensive works was a western style of warfare or lack of anticipation of enemy action is a matter of debate. Grant was accused of being completely surprised when Johnston and Beauregard attacked the Union camps. Virgil's letter to Eliza which follows constitutes some evidence in the matter.

Virgil to Eliza

Pittsburgh, Tenn.
April 9, 1862

Dear Eliza

I suppose as you receive this you will have heard of the great battle of Pittsburgh and maybe you will suppose us all killed or many dire calamaties overtaken us. Thank God we have passed through the greatest battle ever fought in America & nearly all of our company untouched by rebel bullets. Before proceeding to particulars I will tell you of my company tonight. It is Whit, Wall, John, Homer & Rob Medkirk. Whit hunted us up today & Wall just arrived from Nashville today when I was at the river. I came right on to them. You had better believe we had a glorious old meeting all round and a glorious sociable chat tonight.

I will now tell you who are wounded & then give you a history of the battle. I wrote a hasty account to Charley Evans to have published so that persons having friends with me would not feel too uneasy.

34

Our wounded are Geo. Morrison of Napoleon wounded in the shoulder will get well. W. J. Cole of Evansport said to be seriously. I will here state that I have not seen any of them since the fight. They were taken to Savannah on the Boats - F. W. Holtzel slightly on the head, James Myers in the neck, slight, both from Rowels Creek, W. H. Doud, hand, slight, Chris Nagle bad in shoulder, Edwin Cary left arm badly, may have to be taken off. The boys say that Rob Cosgrove has a wound in one leg near ankle. Not very serious. Frank Smith got a spot on left ear that made the blood come. It was a piece of shell that struck him he is doing duty as usual. I believe that is all that were touched. Our sick have been scattered so much that I have been unable to find all since the battle. James Sanders was quite sick. I have not found him yet & don't know where he is. Rob S. is unwell yet, but getting better. Peter Smith was sick & I cannot find him, in fact among so many men it is almost impossible to get track of them but all will come around right in the end for it appears to me that we have been very much favored in this awful battle. I will resume my writing in the morning as the boys have gone to bed & are calling for me. Good night.

Thursday morning, April 10th before breakfast. We have had a good sleep - all in

one bed - & feel first rate this morning &
soon as breakfast is over will feel better as
we have ham, potatoes, tea, etc. Now as I
have given you an account of the wounded &
sick I will proceed to give you an account of
the fight. We had some skirmishing with
them friday and Saturday but none, not even
our Generals expected them to attack us
here, but Sunday morning we, I mean our
tent, had breakfast very early & soon after
the rebels commenced firing on our pickets &
drove them in. We were immediately formed
in line & marched out into the woods & had
been there but a short time until on came the
secesh pell mell firing at us at a distance of
20 rods. They having crossed through a
deep hollow with thick underbrush which was
the reason of their getting so close to us
before we saw them, but our men took them
as they came, each man jumping behind a tree
log or anything else that came handy & then
they commenced in earnest. We fought them
for two hours steady fire. We drove them off
finally but their forces were so much stronger
than ours and were gaining on our left that
we had to retreat. When I speak of our men
I mean our Reg. & that of the 72nd. The
troops on our left gave way soon after the
first fire, that is a number of other
Regiments, say 1/2 to one mile, but had they
stood their ground as our Reg. did we never
would have retreated, but as it was we

retreated two miles but fought all the way. At our first fight on Sunday we had but 10 men killed in all the Reg. We killed over 60 of them in the 2 hour fight and wounded many more. We killed their Gen. Johnson & Bragg, so report says on the very ground we fought over. Tuesday morning I saw Johnson lying on the field near where he fell, his horse also was killed then. If Bragg was killed of which there is but little doubt Jo Kibble done it as he killed an officer with red sash on Jo stood near me. Sunday evening we defended a Battery & lay on our arms all that night without blankets. It rained considerable. My shirts were wet for 3 days but I never felt better in my life than now. Monday morning we marched out and again the fighting commenced. We did not take any active part until about noon when we were in another awful skirmish which lasted an hour. 1 of our captains & 1 man was killed. We drove them back with terrible slaughter. By this time our Col. was wounded & all of our officers scattered so that I was in command of the Reg. until Tuesday evening. By that time we had gathered up some of our officers, Lieutenant Col. etc. Monday evening we came back to our camp and to our regret found everything of value taken or destroyed. I will say here that we were taken so much by surprise Sunday morning that we did not get our trunks saved & had nothing but our

37

everyday clothes on. So you will see by the rebels getting possession of our camp we lost our entire reg. I have nothing left but my blue pants, blouse & old suit, 3 shirts, 4 collars, 1 towel. My entire dress suit including sash, gloves, some shirts & collars, papers, company books & everything in my trunk, my watch and even my little Dud's picture is gone. I hate the loss of the picture and the watch more than all the rest although the value in cash was not so great as the balance. I suppose my real loss is about $70. Twill and Dan lost all their property. Dan lost even his sword. Twill and I had ours. I expect you would kind of laugh was you here to see us without any clothing. Even my stern is almost bare, my pants all ripped and no needle and thread to sew them up with. All the boys are in about the same fix, no blankets, overcoat or clothing of any consequence.

What the rebels could not carry they burnt up. Their retreat was desperate, burning their tents, flour, etc. leaving cannon, wagons etc. etc.

You will get some account in the papers. Get the Cincinnati Times as their reporter was here & will give full particulars. This writing is poor. I cannot help it as my pencil is poor our pens all gone.

Soon as I get a letter from you I will write again. I have not had a letter for 1 week from you. No more at this time only I am very thankful to our protector for preserving us so well in this desperate battle. I forgot to state that the battle extended over about 5 miles of country, mostly in the woods. Yes, my razor is gone too. As Whit is wanting to take my letter to the river I must stop. He wrote to you. Wall says Frank wrote him the best letter & most news of any body that has written to him.

Truly, etc.
V.H.M.
(Virgil H. Moats)

The 'Wall' to whom Virgil refers was his brother, William Wallace Moats. He was 22 years old at the time and a member of Company E of the 14th Ohio Regiment.

'Whit' was Lay Whitney Richardson, Eliza's brother, who was 32 years old at the time, and an officer in the 68th Regiment of Ohio Volunteer Infantry. Two letters from him to Eliza appear later in this volume.

WAR ON THE MISSISSIPPI

While Grant's forces were moving south on the Tennessee to do battle at Shiloh Church, other Union units were moving down the Mississippi. They seized New Madrid, but Rebels at Island 10 on the Mississippi opposite New Madrid still blocked water passage. The flotilla under Flag-Officer A. H. Foote was effective in besieging the Confederate defenders, but a canal had to be cut to bring pressure on the rear. This was successfully accomplished on April 8, 1862 when the garrison of 7000 men surrendered.

As Grant was preparing to move southward toward Corinth, a squadron of sea-going vessels under Flag-officer David A. Farragut was testing Confederate defenses from the south. In action spanning the week of April 18-25, Farragut succeeded in occupying New Orleans. He was unsuccessful in reducing Fort Jackson and Fort St. Philip on the Mississippi that guarded the approaches to the city. He finally made a run past the forts a 2:00 a.m. on the 24th. By the 25th he had sunk Confederate vessels in the vicinity and had occupied New Orleans. Cut off from their supplies, the two forts were forced to surrender.

He was subsequently able to force his way past the defensive batteries at both Port Hudson and Vicksburg. However, he did not have sufficient land forces with him to capture and hold territory. Farragut therefore returned to New Orleans.

SEVEN PINES AND MECHANICSVILLE

In the east maneuvering was occurring in the Valley of Virginia. At Seven Pines or Fair Oaks, McClellan's forces fought a battle on May 31 and June 1 which was similar to the battle of Shiloh. The Union Army of the Potomac was caught unprepared, but after a period of partial losses and a few victories, McClellan managed to form a line and force the Confederates back into the works before Richmond. General J. E. Johnston was severely wounded in this engagement.

Later in June, General Robert E. Lee cut McClellan's lines to the White House with victories at Mechanicsville and Gaines' Mill. However, McClellan managed to change his base and retreat successfully to the James River where there was naval support. However, his attack on Richmond was a strategic failure.

CHRONOLOGY 1862
July to December

BIOGRAPHY		HISTORY
	JULY	
	*	
	AUG.	
VHM to Father	*	
Memphis	*	
VHM to Father	*	
Memphis	*	
	SEPT.	
	* Capture of	
⸙	* Harper's Ferry	
VHM to Eliza	* Battle at	
Sunday Morning	* Antietam	
	OCT.	
VHM to Eliza	* Battle at	
Memphis	* Perrysville	
	NOV.	
VHM to Eliza	*	
Memphis	*	
	DEC.	
VHM to Eliza	* Battle at	
Pickering	* Fredericksburg	
VHM to Eliza	* Battle of Chickasaw	
Steamer Alton	* Bluffs	

Virgil to Eliza

Memphis
Aug. 18 1862

Father

Your letter of Aug. 10 & 11 came today.
I was glad to hear you were all well. Sorry
to hear the boys were under the weather yet.
I am well & no prospect of getting off for
home for the present. I suppose you had not
got my last before you wrote. Do as you think
best with that land any way to save it. That
part to Sanders must be saved. Maybe you had
best pay off the mortgage, & then if the land
sells or any part of it I can see to it, & if
it takes more than $100, I can lay in a claim
for the balance due me. Now have me appointed
Guardian for all the children immediately
before any further advantage is taken. Brown
will charge for his work which we would owe &
thus will be more to make, which might have
been saved, had one of us been appointed.

You have never told me the amount of that
judgment. Do your best & save all you can for
the children, but if the land does sell

I am bound to have it, save money, all after paying judgment, pay none of my debts until this is settled. None of my property can be touched during my absence. I think Eliza has done extremely well. Tell her to save seed Mediterranean clean, & not sell until further notice unless we need the money for buying that land and that will not be very soon. Plenty of time to make arrangements about that, and wheat will not go down in price.

If any bail more than yourself for me as guardian is required, I guess you can get somone there to go it after explaining the matter.

Write soon giving particulars. Make no trouble for yourself about the matter. I must stop as I have a chance to send to Cairo tonight.

None of the last boys have come.

Yours V. H. M.

Since writing the above an idea has come into my head that Lib as she is determined to act mean may be headed a little. Maybe by keeping dark on what I owe Homer, & letting the land sell, paying debts out of proceeds - will cut her out of a portion she claims, by making the amount smaller to be divided with her, and afterwards what I owe can be turned to the children's benefit, as they don't know anything about matters between Homer & me, as there is no note or other account to my knowledge between us & no body else but myself knows how we stand. Nothing in my books about it to my knowledge, & if there is it need not be shown. Do as you think best.

Virgil's father was William Virgil Moats (1799-1881) who lived near Defiance, Ohio.

Homer Moats is listed in the history of Company F as having died in 1862. The stone at Brunersburg, Ohio lists the date as July 21. This letter therefore appears to refer to aspects of the estate of Virgil's brother, Homer and the claims of Homer's wife, Lib.

Virgil to Father

Memphis
Aug. 19, 1862

Father

Since writing you yesterday I have concluded best for Eliza to make that trade with Sanders so that I will have the interest in it myself & If the land can be sold by Sheriff let it be done. As I said yesterday it will make the amount less to be divided with her and leave a larger amount for the children, as nothing need be said about my business with him. You would have to account for amount in your hands, but can put in claim for what you think is due you.

If sheriff cannot sell let it go to Adm. sale as no good will ever come of it until it is sold, as she will always grumble, & the sooner she gets her share the better. A part would have to be sold at any rate, since she makes her claim, in order to pay debts, so best sale of all, and be done with it. Make the best trade with Sanders you can so that he cannot complain.

I don't believe that any person about there can raise the money to buy it. With what I sent last - $220, & my next pay, say $230, which I will get before it can be sold, will make $450. Adding the price of the wheat which can be sold if necessary, making in all near $700, which will be more than enough to buy it. And more than that should I be appointed guardian, I need pay no more than her share & what pays the debts at the time of sale, & what you have of his money & what she gets from Washington will have to be counted in, in paying off herself & the debts. What will be due to the children, I can receipt for, & still have the use of it. So that you see I will have about enough without selling wheat and maybe more than enough.

Don't let any outsiders know anything about our arrangements at present. We can keep our own secrets best. I think this last plan much better than any other that I mentioned before. & She having her own administrator she cannot grumble and no person can say that we cheated her.

Go up soon as you get this & see about matters, & make the trade with Sanders if possible. Let him have that ground for wheat if you think best. Attend to affairs & you can have all you need, so that work need not bother you.

Go up often and see to the seeding.

Write soon V.H.M.

SLAUGHTER AT ANTIETAM
GENERAL HALLECK IS CALLED EAST

Important action was occurring in the east. Lee had sent General Stonewall Jackson to attack and capture Harper's Ferry. This he did on September 15. However, on the 17th, McClelland and the Army of the Potomac attacked Lee's forces in the Battle of Antietam in Maryland. Both sides suffered enormous losses and neither side could really claim to have been victorious. However, General Lee lost ground and moved his forces back into Virginia. As you will see in Virgil's next letter, to the men on the Mississippi, it appeared to be a glorious victory. Although in Washington it was regarded as an expensive failure, Lee was no longer able to take the offensive. From that time on the Confederacy fought a campaign that was almost completely defensive.

In Washington it was decided that McClelland's lack of aggressiveness could no longer be tolerated. Military affairs seemed to be going far better in the west, as indeed they were. Therefore, in September, General

Halleck, who had been in overall charge of operations in the west, was recalled to Washington and placed in supreme command. They were to learn that 'Old Brains,' while a brilliant administrator and organizer, was not the seminal source of successes in the western campaigns.

Virgil to Eliza

Sunday Morning 9 am

We all feel good over the news of Mc-Clellan's success in Maryland, "The Traitor" as the Abolitionists and his enemies call him. I guess he will now shut their unholy mouths & maybe he will have some chance from this on of being let alone, & if so this war will soon be brought to a close. Our boys are on their high horse & you can hear all over camps hurrah for Little Mack, he's the chap, etc., etc. Indeed we do feel good & I rather guess you folks at home feel well also. Now you had better be into the peach & other fruit bearings pretty strongly as I'll want considerable of such articles for filling up when I get home. It will take no small amount to fill us up again. I do think this thing must close out soon. They certainly can't stand many more such whippings as Mack has given them of late, but don't look for us too soon. We will be there soon as possible, you may rest assured of that.

As to you & your old friend, it's all right. I guess he can't do you any damage. "He is too old."

I hardly know what more to write this time only let me know how you get along with the seeding and other work. Have you got your corn cut & is it good. Is Dave Clark cutting his & if not, you must have it done, as we will need all the fodder & other feed raised on the farm. See that all the straw is stacked, & if Bill don't stack that over the creek you find hands & have it done, Sanders's and all. We have not much hay, no more than will be needed for the horses. Consequently, the other feed must be saved for the cattle. About how much hay have you.

While you have a hand hired, & he is not engaged with seeding or cutting corn, etc., or in weather that he can't do such work, you can have chopping done, across the creek opposite the house, or in the bottom below the graveyard. I want all that timber cleared off & all spare time can be put in there & in getting wood for winter etc. Of course you can find plenty to be done, as there is no scarcity of work there. I suppose there is plenty to do yet, cleaning away from about the barn & in the stables. Have work done to the best advantage. How was the oats, & was there any apples on the grafted trees across the creek & if so save some for me to see. We have been living on sweet potatoes for some-time past - plenty of fruit, melons, etc.

Persimmons, grapes & nuts in abundance, but yet living is very high.

Yours
V. H. M.

This undated letter appears to have been written Circa September 25, 1862.

BUELL AND BRAGG IN KENTUCKY

While Grant was occupied in central Mississippi, the Confederates made a move out of Tennessee into Kentucky. General Braxton Bragg sent General Kiley Smith to Lexington and then moved his main force out of Chattanooga and into Kentucky. General Buell just managed to get his forces between the Confederates and the Ohio River. Grant and General William S. Rosecrans fought off attacks at Iuka and Corinth and sent aid to Buell.

A battle between Buell and Bragg occurred at Perrysville, Kentucky more or less by accident. Neither had planned a battle there, but the two armies blundered into each other on October 8, and the slaughter typical of the Civil War ensued. Bragg decided to withdraw back into Tennessee and Buell declined to follow up and pursue him. As a result of this failure, Buell was removed and replaced by General Rosecrans who then moved his forces into Nashville.

Memphis, Tenn.
Oct. 2, 1862

Dear Eliza:

I am well and hope you and all are the same. I thought best to write you a few lines to let you know how I am getting along and to inquire after you and family. No letter from you since the one dated Sept. 7th. Can't tell why I don't get letters. Others have been getting letters yesterday and today up to as late as Sept. 25 less than a week. Are you or any of the rest sick that you don't write or what is the matter. I have the blues the worst kind about it can't content myself at anything just thinking of you. Is Father sick yet.

We have had some trouble in our company. Henry Doud went crazy and with all our watching not considering him dangerous nor noticing anything vicious, we had not tied him. Monday morning he caught hold of a gun & ran the bayonet into his brother, Ed, who was lying down on his bunk close by watching him. He done it so quick that none could prevent it although several stood by. The bayonet went through the right arm above the elbow behind the bone & into his right breast. Supposed at the time to have penetrated to his lung, but now such is not supposed to have been the case, as his breathing or talking is not interferred with. The wound was a very serious one & was at the time thought fatal, but now we have no fears of his case, as he rests well and talks freely as usual. Henry has been failing ever since, he is very poorly. We expect to start him for Dayton this day. I feel very bad at the occurrence, but all in our power was done to prevent such a catastrophe. They have always been good boys and I hate to lose them from the company, but such are the some of the casualties of this desparate war. I know no particular cause of Henry's derangement. All he says now is in reference to Jeff. Davis and Lincoln's proclamation which he appears very much opposed to.

Our boys pay good attention to them & stays with them night and day. John R is now asleep having been up with Ed all night.

Most of our boys are well. None in the hospital but Douds.

I guess I have written about all for this time.

Oh I have heard that some trouble has or did occur among the Mocks, that something was wrong about his medicine or in giving them to him, that a quarrel was the result, etc., etc., that (Isaac) made a will and if so what did it amount to, & is he dead and to whom did he will his property. (This is private don't mention it) but give me the particulars.

In my last I sent Dud a speech. If you got it tell me how he makes it go. I made a mistake. It should be, The butcher killed a calf, and that's half, & so on. (I left out - "and that's half.")

Love to all.

No more for this time.

Good Bye   V.H.M.

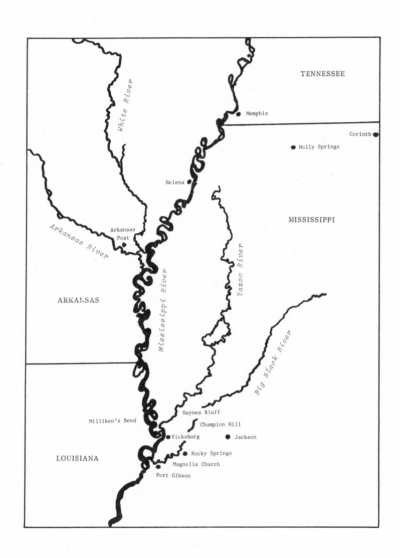

TENNESSEE

Memphis

Corinth

Holly Springs

Helena

MISSISSIPPI

Arkansas
Post

White River

Arkansas River

Mississippi River

Yazoo River

Big Black River

ARKANSAS

LOUISIANA

Milliken's Bend

Haynes Bluff

Champion Hill

Vicksburg   Jackson

Rocky Springs

Magnolia Church

Port Gibson

Focus on Vicksburg

FOCUS ON VICKSBURG

When Union forces in the west began their southward advance from Illinois, Missouri and Kentucky in February 1862, one of their objectives was to achieve command of the Mississippi. In so doing they could reestablish commercial navigation from St. Louis to the sea, and in the process separate the western states of the Confederacy from those east of the river.

At Shiloh they had begun to move south on a path that could lead to an attack on Vicksburg from the east and thus from the land side. In pursuit of this strategy, Grant assembled an army of more than 100,000 men and moved on Corinth. Beauregard with 50,000 had to retire to central Mississippi.

At the same time, Union gunboats destroyed a Confederate fleet at Memphis, and two months after Shiloh, Memphis had to be abandoned. But in the autumn Union forces came to a standstill and were called upon to repulse the counter-advance of the Southern armies.

The Confederates remained in control of a substantial length of the Mississippi. This stretch began at Helena, just below Memphis in the north. It included fortifications at Arkansas Post near the mouth of the Arkansas River, those at Vicksburg, and more at Port Hudson between New Orleans and Vicksburg. It was to be the task of Grant's army, then around Corinth, and the flotilla of gunboats then at Memphis to destroy this system of defenses and join hands with Farragut, thus clearing the whole course of the Mississippi.

Of these three, Vicksburg, Arkansas Post and Port Hudson, Vicksburg was to be the most difficult to approach. At Vicksburg there is a system of bluffs which leave the Mississippi to follow the course of the Yazoo before rejoining the great river at Memphis. Therefore, Vicksburg could be approached via the uplands east of the river, or from the west through the maze of bayous, backwaters and side channels. The land to the west was swampy but kept dry by levees in some places near the river.

There were thus two obvious ways to approach Vicksburg. Grant's forces could come from Corinth and approach from the east via Granada, or try to attack via the river and through the bayous. The Confederate

Army under General J. C. Pemberton, which was in the field north and east of Vicksburg, could front either north against an advance by Granada or west along the bluffs above and below Vicksburg. The rear of Vicksburg, the east and south side, was less defensible. A Union approach in this sector was very much to be preferred.

In pursuit of this approach, Grant moved from Corinth to Holly Springs with a force of 40,000 men who could be spared from other duties, established a base and prepared to move on Granada.

McCLERNAND'S POLITICAL MANEUVER

As Grant was preparing to execute his plan he began to hear rumors that there was a campaign to take Vicksburg by a force moving down the Mississippi - a plan of which he knew nothing. It gradually developed that General McClernand had gone to Washington and obtained permission, virtually in secret, to raise his own army in the north, an army he was to command. There would be a combined army-navy direct assault on Vicksburg.

To foil McClernand, Grant ordered General Sherman to take charge in Memphis and to incorporate McClernand's troop levees as they appeared, and move south to Milliken's Bend and Young's Point a few miles above Vicksburg. This he did with 30,000 men.

Memphis, Nov. 16

Well Eliza

No letter from you for some time. Your letter that you said you would write two weeks ago today has not yet come to hand. May be you forgot it.

I have not much to write only to tell you that we are well as usual. McFeters is improving some. John Johnson is doing very well.

Got a letter from Father the other day.

I will write soon as I hear from you. Our things have not yet come. I fear they were on the boat that sunk Wednesday night - The Eugene & may be lost. The letter I got was wet - was on that boat. Write soon & keep me posted. No pay yet poor prospects for it soon.

Don't tell any person that I want to buy that land. Let on as though we don't intend to buy it. I want to beat some of them if possible.

Brown and Lib are trying to get all, even the land. They must not have it, if it can be prevented.

Write soon

Yours etc   V. H. M.

Are the boys, Clint & all well and how do they all flourish.

VIRGIL

War Department records show that Virgil
was detached from his unit sometime in
November and sent by General Sherman to
Columbus, Kentucky on special business. It
seems quite possible that the business at
hand related to the movement and handling of
the troops that General McClernand was
raising in Illinois. The records also show
that Virgil was Acting Garrison Adjutant at
Fort Pickering from December 5th through
December 20th.

FREDERICKSBURG

At the end of November General A. E. Burnside with an Army of the Potomac numbering 122,000 men was positioned before Fredericksburg where Lee's forces, numbering 78,500, were dug into defensive positions. Burnside's goal was to crush the Confederate Army before him and move on to take Richmond.

Union forces opened the battle on December 11th, and within the next two days engineers had bridged the Rappahannock in three places. Union forces poured into the lowlands and into the town itself. On the 13th Federal forces were separated from Confederate positions on Marye's Heights by two small bridges and an open field in front of the Stone Wall and sunken road. The only approach to the enemy was through these confining hazards. The Union position was militarily untenable and the Confederate position virtually impregnable. Repeated assaults left heaps of Federal bodies sufficient in number to serve as protection for soldiers behind them. It is estimated that 9000 Union men died before Marye's Heights, while Confederate losses were about 1500.

During the night of December 13-14, General Burnside became convinced that further action was useless, and he ordered his army to retreat back across the river. Another attempt to move on Richmond had been turned away with enormous losses in human lives on both sides.

It was while observing the action from a position above Fredericksburg that General Lee was heard to comment, "It is well that war is so terrible - we should grow too fond of it."

THE WAR ON VICKSBURG

Grant knew, but was officially uninformed, that McClernand had convinced Washington authorities that Vicksburg was best attacked via the river. In pursuit of his own plan to attack primarily from the southeast, he undertook to move before McClernand could appear with official orders. He ordered Sherman to attack from the river side while he simultaneously attacked from the east.

The first advance was made on Granada at the end of November 1862 by two columns from Grand Junction and Memphis. The Confederates in the field, greatly outnumbered, fell back without fighting. But Grant's line of supply was one long single-line, ill-equipped railway through Grand Junction to Columbus. Confederate cavalry under Van Dorn swept around his flank and destroyed one of his principal magazines at Holly Springs, and without further effort compelled the abandonment of the advance. Bedford Forrest with another cavalry unit cut rail lines to the north and captured even more of the precious supplies.

Grant was unable to get word to Sherman that the approach from the rear had been temporarily halted. As a consequence, Sherman attempted to carry out his prong of the two-prong attack. This was unfortunate as we shall later see.

Virgil to Eliza

Hd. Quarters Fort Picking
Dec. 20th 1862

Dear Eliza

I write you a few lines to let you know that I am well & expect to leave here by tomorrow. By some unaccountable reason we have been ordered off. We go down the River. I will draw pay & send it today by express, also send my trunk and cot. I hate very much to leave my good position but such is the fate of war. All uncertainty. You will keep the money until you hear from me again which will be soon & often. I may write more before I leave. Do not be uneasy about me. I will try & take care of myself. Trust in God and all will be well.

Since writing the above the Gen. has pressed Gen. Hurlbut to have me remain with him but they won't allow it so I will have to go. Gen. Asboth is wrathy about me having to leave him, & I don't like it very well myself. I may get another good place. The boys were

71

very much opposed to my remaining behind. I
have to write by spells. Must stop a while.

I will mail this. No money yet. Will
probably be paid before we leave. I sent my
trunk, my Shiloh blouse. Take care of it & in
vest pocket find a nice watch for yourself.
Had no time nor money to get picture. Will
write soon.

Good bye   V. H. M.

Virgil to Eliza

On board Steamer City of Alton
below Helena
Monday, Dec. 22, 1862

Dear Eliza

Yesterday about two o'clock our fleet composed of about 50 boats all loaded with soldiers with the addition of about 20 gunboats & mortars left Memphis for, well I don't know where, probably Vicksburg, maybe Yazoo River. We passed Helena about 10 miles and laid up for the night -- started this morning about 10 & are now making fine headway down the broad Mississippi. We are having a fine trip & I hope a successful one without danger, but then you know war is always attended with danger. What we are going for I can't tell but expect to take Vicksburg. Our coming away from Memphis was rather against our feelings. Nearly all were oppsd. to it & we blame our Lt. Col. for it. Col. Sullivan is not on duty on account of his arm and did not come with us. Lt. Col. Parker got us started & all are down on him for it, he was very keen to get us started & will be the first to start back when danger threatens. We were so well fixed at Memphis, indeed no soldier could have asked for better treatment, it was as near home in comfort as we could have expected & besides that our communications with home was very good & that is no small matter with me. All say better let good enough alone & hope Parker will get his satisfaction before he gets through. I would hate to have the curses he gets for coaxing Gen. Hurlbut to allow him to trade with another regt., it taking our place in the fort that we might hold until spring well as not.

Well, enough of that for the present, you will hear more of it hereafter. Now for something else I met with bad luck Friday night in going from Head Quarters to the Co. I was somewhat out of humor at hearing of our moving & not paying much attention to where I was going, stepped on a snag and tore the right leg of my new breeches very bad, almost spoiling them, but I guess I can get them fixed so as to do pretty well. You had better believe it made me mad & had I been in the habit of swearing might have cussed Parker a little, but then you know your old boy V. never does such things, & ain't you glad of that. War with all its vices don't cause me to swear. Who would not have got mad at leaving such a good place as we all had & such a place as mine was in particular, even the old General Asboth was mad about it. I could have remained with him all winter had our regt. stayed. Well that was not all of my bad luck. We got our pay after we got on the boat Saturday night about 2 o'clock and of course I had to break a little piece off the Sabbath in going up town to send my money, and while there I thought best to get a picture & send as you requested. So I got it and went to the Express office to send it and on coming out of the door slipped and fell getting all mud, hurting my back and nearly breaking my arm. I really don't know whether it was just bad luck or for breaking the Sabbath, but at any rate I was out of humor & at the time would not have cared much if I had broken a bone then I could have stayed behind, and gone home. Now I hope you will think none the less of the picture, because it was taken on that day nor none the less of the original for having it done, as that was the best I could do & I know you & the boys wanted the picture no difference when taken, & I expect would like to see the old chap himself even with a broken arm. The cost was $5 and ain't that high? We left behind on account of sore eyes principally, Hockman, McFeeters, Carroll & Rath, Geo. Hopkins to be discharged and Edwards to take care of sick of the regt. I wanted John Johnson to stay behind but he would not since he was bound to go along, he is getting along very well and fleshing up, none are sick.

We had to send our trunks and things home being unable to carry any thing but a satchel. My old trunk & things were hardly worth sending but I think so much of them that I could not bear to throw them away & besides my blankets and other things I could not carry were to good to throw away, on the whole we won't lose much by sending them home. My blouse that I wore at Shiloh take good care of & the watch get a chrystal & key for & have for yourself, it is a good one & with a nice chain will be pretty for a _lady_ to carry. Maybe you will say that you are not a lady. Any good woman is a lady and no other, fine clothes don't always make the real lady, do you think so? It is getting dark in my room. I must stop until after supper & then write more. The boat shakes so bad that I can hardly write, hope you can read it however.

Tuesday morning 23rd have just passed Napoleon. I promised to write last night but could not & now the boat shakes so bad that I can hardly write. I will quit writing for this time hoping to be able to write with more comfort after a while. I can do better with a pencil & will write on for a time at any rate. I expect we will meet Whit somewhere below &

now I will tell you that I believe that we are going up Yazoo River get the map and you will see that it puts into the Miss just above Vicksburg 12 miles. Grant's Army and ours will meet there, that is the opinion of many at any rate. I have not much to write about home matters having written all that was necessary in my former letters.

The last money I sent keep until we see how that land matter terminates. We will not buy unless it sells cheap & I will be so far away that we cannot well correspond on the subject with certainty. Soon as it is appraised write to me giving the appraisment and then I can tell you what to do. Write two letters close together answering it so that I may get one at least. I will be very likely to get a letter from you the first mail that comes down after us. Monday was the day that it should have come but then we were on the river & no mail.

When I will get to send this is hard to tell, it may be a week or more. I think we will reach our destination tomorrow evening & it may not be long before some of the boats go back up the river. Now you will have to write often if you expect me to hear from you at all as I will be along ways from you. Vicksburg is 400 miles below Memphis. As I have filled this sheet I will stop for this time promising more before it starts.

The first part of this letter was written in pen. It was finished in pencil.

AN ABORTED ATTACK ON VICKSBURG

Virgil's guess about where they were going turned out to be pretty good. Following Grants' plan, Sherman with a flotilla of boats and some 30,000 men prepared to attack Vicksburg fron the water side, while Grant was assumed to be dealing with the Confederate field army on the high ground. As we know, but Sherman didn't, Van Dorn had cut Grant's line of supply. Thus the Confederate army was free to turn on Sherman. The latter, ignorant of Grant's predicament, attacked the Yazoo heights above Vicksburg in the Battle of Chickasaw Bluffs on December 29th. But a large portion of Pemberton's field army had arrived to help defend the Vicksburg garrison, and the Federals were easily repulsed with a loss of 1700 men. Major Virgil described the action in his next letter. Note the discrepancy between Virgil's casualty figures and those of the count of 1700 reported in historical accounts.

1863

Virgil to Eliza

On board Steamer City of Alton
January 3, 1863

Dear Eliza and family

Again I write you a short letter to let you know where I am & that I am yet alive & among the living. My health & that of the boys is good although we have had some pretty hard times since I last wrote - which was on this boat & I hope you got it

We arrived at the mouth of Yazoo Saturday 27th & landed in the evening, laid on the boat during the night & was on the march before day for Vicksburg. Our advance had been skirmishing with rebels on the left since Friday. Sunday morning fighting was very severe in that direction. We kept on our way until we came in sight of their fortifications on the hills to the right - or up the river from the city where we halted, & also where they had cut down all the timber to impede our progress. We remained in that position during the day & in the evening fell back about two miles and encamped.

The rebels did not open on us although in full view and not more than one half-mile distant.

We remained in our encampment until Wednesday morning when we went on picket, & during the day the reb picket showed a flag of truce & we met them half way on the river bank above the city - and within 80 rods of their batteries - had a nice chat - talked over matters, agreed not to fire on each other while on picket, & finally parted on the best of terms, that they all saying they were heartily tired of the war. They were East Tennesseans, & I know they were for several of them had deserted & come over the two previous nights & they were taken off picket that night and others put in their place - for fear they would desert. Those that came over said that whole companies of their regiment would come at the first opportunity. That is the feeling in nearly all their regiments.

Thursday Gen. Sherman finding them too strong for him being unable to make any very considerable impression on their works - although he succeeded in taking two of their forts - & Gen. Grant & other expected assistance failing to appear as understood, he was compelled to fall back & take the boats. Accordingly during the night our artillery teams, baggage etc. were all sent back & at two in the morning we were on our way & before

84

daylight were on the boat - distance from where we landed to City about 9 miles. Friday after we left the rebels shelled the woods severely but we were not there. There shells did no harm except to destroy timber. The country over which we passed is low bottom & all woods & when the water is up covers it to a depth of 15 feet. The weather while in there was warm days cold nights freezing so as to make ice. It is a fine thing we got out for the rain commenced falling yesterday afternoon and continued to fall in torrents all night, & by this time the bottom must be covered.

We are now at Milliken bend where I finished my last letter. What we will do next, where we will go, or when we will leave here is more than I can tell. I believe that I have given you all the particulars, and all that has transpired since my last.

Our loss in the fighting was about 160 killed, 200 wounded, none in our brigade.

I will stop for this time. May write more before this goes. I am so nervous & write so poor that I fear you will hardly be able to read this, but you must over look that for this time. You had best save all my letters for the present. They may be of some account sometime. Since writing the above I learn that we land now as rain is over and that the boats go up river & that mail will go to morrow. So I will close for this time & will write again soon. Write twice a week and give one all the news.

I have no instructions to give only do the best you can with everything. I have not received any letters from home since we left Memphis.

Good bye for this time will write longer next time.

V.H.M.
(Virgil H. Moats)

(John Johnson is
getting fat as a
pig.)

CHRONOLOGY 1863
January to June

BIOGRAPHY	HISTORY
	JAN.
VHM to Eliza	* Emancipation
Steamer Alton	* Proclamation
LWR to Eliza	* Battle of
Near Vicksburg	* Murphreesburg
VHM to Eliza	* Fall of
Arkansas Post	* Arkansas Post
VHM to Eliza	*
Opposite Vicksburg	*
	FEB.
Appointed Major	*
	MAR.
	*
	APR.
VHM to Eliza	*
Headquarters	*
	MAY
VHM to Eliza	* Battle of
Rocky Springs	* Chancellorsville
	* Pemberton driven
	* into Vicksburg
	* Failed Assaults
VHM Wounded	* on Vicksburg
	JUNE
VHM Granted Leave	*
JR to VHM	*
Near Vicksburg	*

THE POLITICS OF WAR IN WASHINGTON

It was shortly after the action at Chickasaw Bayou that Lincoln issued the Emancipation Proclamation on the first of January, 1863. While slavery had been an issue all along, the war had been fought primarily to save the Union. With the issuance of the proclamation, the freeing of the slaves became a figural objective of the Northern war effort.

ROSECRANS AT MURPHREESBURG

Back in Tennessee, Confederate General Bragg with 37,000 men took up a position near Murphreesburg. Rosecrans soon followed and on December 31st his men fought an inclusive but bloody battle on frozen fields before Bragg's position. The fighting recurred daily until January 3 at which point Bragg withdrew. Rosecrans lost 13,000 men and Bragg an estimated 12,000, roughly 30 percent of each army.

THE ARKANSAS POST EXPEDITION

General McClernand finally arrived on January 2 from his recruiting forays into Illinois, and he was frustrated and furious because Grant would not let him proceed with the plan he had developed on his own. At this point Sherman proposed an expedition to destroy the Confederate garrison at Arkansas Post before attempting fresh operations against Vicksburg. Virgil and the 48th Ohio Volunteer Infantry were a part of Sherman's forces.

Immediately after McClernand and the last of his new recruits arrived at Milliken's Bend, on January 4th, the expedition set out. It was jointly commanded by Sherman and McClernand and was sent on the same transport boats on which McClernand had arrived. The expedition was escorted by Porter's gunboats. Arkansas Post occupied the site of an old settlement on the north bank of the Arkansas River, fifty miles from its mouth. Situated on a high bluff at the head of a horseshoe bend of the river, the fort was described as a very strong work. It was strongly armed and garrisoned by 5000 men under General Churchill, who had been directed to hold the place until the last man was dead.

The Union forces proceeded up the White River and through the cut-off to the Arkansas. They disembarked on the evening of the 9th and on the next day moved to attack the fort. Early on January 11th, Sherman got his forces into position to attack but waited until the gunboats could get into position to fire. The battle began at one p.m. The enemy did not reply, and shortly thereafter, Sherman ordered his columns forward. The infantry dashed across about one hundred yards of open ground, and then reached a strip about three hundred yards wide that was much cut up with gulleys and covered with timber, underbrush and logs. They encountered withering fire from the enemy, and their advance was slowed. By three o'clock they were within a hundred yards of the enemy's entrenchments, and Porter's gunboats were close to the fort. The fight raged on for another hour. At four o'clock the enemy raised white flags all along the line. Sherman entered the fort to discuss the surrender with General Churchill. Firing was heard and it was reported that General Deshler, who commanded a brigade of Rebels, had refused to surrender because he had received no order to do so from General

Churchill. Sherman and Churchill moved to quiet the disturbance, and when they reached Deshler, he was persuaded to surrender and ordered his men to stack arms.

The Union loss was 129 killed, 831 wounded and 17 missing. General Churchill reported 75-80 wounded, and an unknown number killed, but the Confederate loss was thought to be much greater. The fort, its 5000 defenders and a considerable supply of arms were captured on the 11th of January 1863. The prisoners were sent to St. Louis.

McClernand, elated at what he regarded as his victory, would have continued to ascend the Arkansas River, but such an eccentric operation would have been profitless if not dangerous, and Grant, authorized by General Halleck who was general-in-chief, preemptorily ordered McClernand back to the Mississippi.

Virgil to Eliza

Dear Eliza and family

I again write you a few lines to let you know of my whereabouts which you will learn from the caption of this letter. We have just been through an other terrific battle, & thank God I and all the boys except Geo Blair are safe & sound. Poor George was killed, the ball passing through or near his heart he spoke but a part of a sentence after he was struck. One of the boys by his side asked him where he was shot his reply was, "I don't know where" & immediately expired without a groan. We feel his loss as he was one of our very best boys, & as brave as good he was clear in the advance when killed. We buried him as best we could, making a very nice box.

When I wrote you last we were at the mouth of White River & on Thursday Friday started & followed that stream a few miles until we came to where there is a connection between that & this river, & crossed through it, & followed it to near this place same day about (30) miles, both rivers are narrow, crooked & deep, but few places wide enough for our large boats to turn. Saturday morning landed some troops on opposite side to this place & then moved up within two miles, disembarked afternoon, & after night came up within half mile of the Fort. Sunday morning preparations made for attacking. Everything ready by 12 o'c noon. Gun boats moved up & opened on their heavy guns at the same our artillery opening all along their line which was near one mile in length. by half past one all their guns 10 in number were silenced & musketry fighting commenced, & by half past three their works were in our possession. At about half past two our regt. opened fire having been some earlier ordered forward to support as a reserve some other regts. finally getting orders to advance broke across an open field to within 300 yards of their intrench-ments, fell down for a short time in a hollow, & here our Lt. Col. Parker got a severe shot in the left arm injuring bone below the elbow. Command then devolved on Capt. Peterson and myself. We ordered it forward. The boys up & yelling their best run about 100 yds, running entirely over the 16th Ind. then being inside of 200 yds of the works, again fell down allowing their balls to pass entirely over us. We then opened fire loading while laying on the ground behind bushes, logs, fences etc. In this position we worked until they surren-dered nearly one hour. It was here that George was killed, having got clear ahead of

94

all, - with one or two exceptions - & on his knees loading. They raised their white flags in token of surrender off to our right. We then raised up & those rebs in front not seeing the white flags fired on us without effect causing us to lie down again but soon the truce flag appeared in front, & again to our feet, & then commenced one of the greatest runs you ever heard of for the fort & owing to some trouble in getting into line we were beaten by one other regt. who succeeded in planting their flag first on their works, although we were the nearest of any other regt. Our success was all that could be desired, & in part atoned for our ill success at Vicksburg. Our prisoners amount to about 6000 - none escaping - & the loss on our side about 500 killed & wounded. Their loss in killed and wounded small being well protected by their works. The loss in our regt. is surprisingly small considering our exposed position only two killed 13 wounded none very seriously.

Our boys behaved admirably & Company F can't be beaten, cowards are scarce in it. I feel proud of them & had we suffered no loss, no feelings of regret need mar our comfort as soldiers.

This is Monday night. I am on the Boat writing. The boys are in the fort ½ mile off. Some of our boys are yet on the boat & were not in the fight. John E. Richardson has been having the ague hard & was not out. Jason has very sore eyes & was not out. Andrew Smith, Nagel, Kellogg & Butler, not very well, were none of them out.

I have not much further to write. I have given you the particulars of the fight & will say further that while it lasted Shiloh was nowhere.

No letters yet from you, don't blame you. Suppose you have written often enough but the rebs got our large mail of ours as I wrote you once before.

There has a mail gone out to the Regt. Maybe a letter for me, but I can't wait for it as the mail goes in the morning. Should I get one I'll write again.

I expect we will go back to the Miss. River as the water is to low for us to go to Little Rock at this time.

My own health is not very good. I caught a severe cold in my head which is rather troublesome for comfort. I will be all right in a day or two.

Will write soon again

Direct your letters to 48th OV. Army Miss. Gen. Morgan's Corps. Army Miss.

Good night
V. H. M.

While this letter is dated 1862, the events described occurred in 1863. Who hasn't perseverated into the new year with the old date?

ATTEMPTS TO SOLVE
THE VICKSBURG PROBLEM

Grant had sailed down the river and joined McClernand and Sherman at Milliken's Bend and assumed command at the beginning of February. At this point the army under Grant was divided into four divisions commanded by Generals McClernand, Sherman, Hurlbut, and McPherson, and he had the cooperation of the flotilla under Captain David D. Porter. Feeling restricted in his approach to Vicksburg because of McClernand's maneuvers in Washington, Grant tried several approaches to the reduction of the Vicksburg garrison.

First Grant tried to cut a canal across the bend of the Mississippi near Vicksburg. He hoped to isolate the fortress, gain a water connection with the lower river, and land an army on the bluffs beyond Pemberton's left flank. This was unsuccessful because the river perversely refused to enter the new channel in any volume.

Next he tried to cut a channel from the Mississippi to Lake Providence and to the upper Yazoo and thereby to expose Pemberton's right. This plan failed because he was unable to obtain a sufficient number of the shallow-draft boats necessary to carry out this operation.

There was a plan to cut the levee 300 miles north and deepen small streams to give access to the Yazoo. The Confederates, warned in time, constructed Fort Pemberton at the point from which Grant's advance would emerge from the bayous.

Lastly he tried an advance through Steele's bayou, a maze of creeks leading toward the middle Yazoo and Haynes's Bluff. There they encountered the enemy, not on the bluffs, but in the low-lying woods and islands. These Confederates harassed and delayed the progress of the expedition so effectively that Grant recalled his forces.

Virgil to Eliza

Dear Eliza

    I write you a few lines to let you know I am and how I am getting along. You will see by the heading where we are and we are opposite to the town west side of the river & in full view of the city. As to my health it is not very good but better than it has been. After I wrote to you while near Ark. Post. I was taken with a kind of chill fever which lasted several days. I was 4 days without taking a bite. After getting some better I took cold which settled into my neck causing quinsy. I was 3 days without swallowing anything but a little water & that with great difficulty & pain. My mouth & tongue was awful, tongue so swollen that my mouth stood wide open for two days & black as coles. Now I feel pretty well although my throat is some sore yet but I can swallow very well, & have a good appetite. Although very much reduced in flesh, I just came to camp today having stayed on the boat to keep from catching cold. I could have had a furlough for 20 days to go to Memphis had I been able to get around, but it would not have done me much good as I could not have got home. I don't want any more such spells. If I do have I'll break for the North where all white men ought to be.

Our expenses have been so great that my money is all gone. You see that I have been 6 weeks on boats nearly all the time. Now don't be scared about me I will get along all right & would have written before this had I been able. Since I got your letter of Jan. 4th the one of Dec. 29 came. I will not write much this time. The boys have had a very hard time on boat & in camp nearly all were ailing more or less. Frank Smith had a very hard time with Eresypelas in his face but is getting better. Bill is on boat sick with fever contracted while taking care of Frank. Geo Minsel is also on boat sick. The others are all in camp.

Since I commenced this I got a letter written by Whit while at our house, & it made me about half mad it was so short, good what there was of it, but he didn't say how he got home or anything about it or whether he was going back or not.

Neither did you or Clint think it worth while to write a word.

I wrote that those Rec'd notes were in the house among my papers.

I also wrote to keep clear of any difficulty with these folks and not to buy a horse but save the money until I direct its use.

Jake Snyder, Geo. Nostel, Ike Ridenour and Eugene Brant have left us & the other boys say they have deserted. I did not think they would do it but I hope they will get through safely. They left below Napoleon Ark. I fear they will have a hard time in getting through.

I will close for this time. Hoping to hear from you soon. I will write again soon.

Good bye
V. H. Moats

My letter to the Democrat I did not get finished before taken sick. I will not send it now.

VIRGIL

In a letter dated February 18, to Colonel
D. P. Grier from Captain S. G. W. Peterson,
the following request was made:

"Sir:

*Capt. V. H. Moats, Co. Fetter's Regiment,
having made application, based on Surgeon's
Certificate of Disability, for leave of
absence, and same having been thereby for-
warded to Department Hd. Qrs, at which place
it was endorsed with leave to go to Memphis
and started on its return to the Regiment, but
from some cause having failed to reach him and
he still being in exceedingly poor health, I
would most respectfully ask that he be granted
leave of absence for twenty days for the
purpose of recruiting his health as well as
attending to business for the Regiment in
looking for deserters and absentees there-
from."*

The leave was granted by General Grant
and it was apparently extended several times.
As mentioned in the letter to follow, he
seemed to be able, during this time, to

return home for a short furlough. While he was reported to be present with the regiment in March, he did not return to the regiment at Milliken's Bend until April 9. He was promoted from Captain to Major on April 10, with the advancement made retroactive to February 21, 1863. He returned to active duty on April 11.

THE FINAL PLAN TO TAKE VICKSBURG

After his unsuccessful efforts on the
north side, Grant decided to undertake the
maneuvers at the rear of Vicksburg which
were finally to be successful and which
established his reputation. He spent most of
the spring working out the details of the
campaign.

Union Gunboat

The troops marched overland from Milliken's Bend to New Carthage, and on the 16th of April, Porter ran his gunboat flotilla and three laden transports past the batteries. Several days later he took five more transports and twelve barges past the fortifications successfully, even though there was considerable damage done to the barges. With supplies now below Vicksburg on the Louisiana side, it was then possible to move troops south to Hard Times Landing from which they crossed to the Mississippi side.

All of this, which involved careful arrangement and hard work, was done by the 24th of April. General N. P. Banks, with a Union army from New Orleans, was now advancing up the river to attack Port Hudson, a Confederate stronghold well below Vicksburg.

By way of diverting attention away from the Mississippi, a Confederate cavalry brigade under Benjamin Grierson rode 600 miles in 16 days to reach Baton Rouge, destroying railways and magazines and cutting the telegraph wires en route. Grant was not impressed.

Virgil to Eliza

Dear Eliza

As I have a little leisure this afternoon I will improve the opportunity by writing you a short letter. I stated in my letter that accompanied the money, which I sent the 14th that we were about to leave Millikens Bend which we did Wednesday 15th reaching this place - Holmes farm - yesterday afternoon only stopping over night at Richmond. We are now about 18 miles from the bend, rather below Vicksburg & about 12 miles from Carthage on the river below.

The intention of this move I think is to cut off all communication the Rebs have with the West crippling their supplies effectually from that source. Some say we are going to cross the river below to get into the rear of the rebels at Vicksburg, which I doubt. A great portion of the country is flooded, all between us & Vicksburg is covered with water, and we are only protected by a levee along a bayou. Every thing in the shape of a stream

107

in this country has to be kept in by levees. The whole country back is lower than the river when high, and when the water breaks through it tears everything crazy in running back into the swamps & bayous.

The planters through here don't appear to be doing much in the farming line. Although we have passed some splendid plantations. Corn is large enough to cultivate, roses & other flowers in full bloom, peaches large as plums, & right here I saw today peas ready to blossom, but the whole country is stripped of everything, & the lady at the house wants to get flour of the boys, & says she has had none for months, neither salt, coffee or anything else or the niceties & comforts of civilized life.

You ladies at home enjoying all of the comforts of life sometimes grumble about your hard fare, but how do you think you would like to live as these people do with a large farm & nothing to live upon but cornbread & meat without salt. I rather think there would be some tall grumbling, don't you?

Well enough of that. As to a fight at Vicksburg I think it very doubtful. I believe the rebs after they see their supplies cut off will get out of the way fast as possible leaving the place to us. I hope so at least.

The weather is quite warm, about like it is at home in June, it rather draws the sweat out of me fat as I am. My health is pretty good as you would guess from the profile I sent with the money. My cough has stopped entirely, & I believe I am fatter than ever. The trip home rather agreed with me than otherwise, - maybe it agreed with you too, - the boys rib me about being so big.

I reckon some people's curiosity will be satisfied when they hear of the $600. Don't gratify them if you can avoid it. I sent the money as I did to John so that Phillip could not circulate it all over the country. I don't wish everyone to know how much we have, as it is none of their business, it is our own & no other persons. The boys are generally well No news lately from Bill Smith. Laser is here to day.

I fear mail may not be very regular, therefore I will write often & you must do the same. It is time I had one from you. I don't know how long we will stay here maybe not very long.

The boys must raise lots of potatoes, melons etc. as I will try & be at home in time for them. How does Dud's pigs flourish, does he feed them any yet. All the boys must be good & attend to things right. I will quit for this time, & will write soon again.

Good bye

V. H. Moats

You need not pay Bill Gunsaullus back that $15. I will settle it with Dan here.

The 'Dan' with whom Virgil promised to settle accounts, is Daniel Gunsaullus who is mentioned in the Postcript on the 48th Ohio Volunteer Infantry toward the end of this book.

GETTING BEHIND VICKSBURG

Virgil was wrong on at least three counts. The river was crossed to get to the rear of Vicksburg; there was fighting to come at Vicksburg; and Virgil's hopes were not fulfilled that the Rebels would quit when they saw that their source of supplies was cut off.

On April 29th Grant resolved to attack Grand Gulf to the south of Vicksburg. Sherman was sent north to divert rebel troops on Haynes Bluff on the Yazoo. The attacks occurred on April 30th. On the same day, McClernand crossed the Mississippi followed by McPherson. The nearest Confederate brigades, attempting to oppose the advance at Port Gibson, were driven back. Several battles occurred involving the men of both McPherson and Sherman. Pemberton with 25,000 Confederate troops was now at Vicksburg and sallied out to attack Grant, but Grant attacked this force at Edward's Depot and induced it to retire back into Vicksburg.

CHANCELLORSVILLE

It was April and in the narrow gap between Washington and Richmond the Army of the Potomac was preparing again to attack Lee and drive its way to Richmond. This time the man in command was General Joseph Hooker, and he had more than 120,000 men at his disposal. Lee had a defensive force scarcely half as strong, approximately 60,000 men. On May 1st Hooker was moving his army toward Fredericksburg for yet another try. In mid-movement he lost his nerve and pulled back into Chancellorsville. In the battle there he was out-maneuvered and defeated by Lee and General Stonewall Jackson. Hooker lost 17,000 men in the process.

While the battle was clearly a Confederate victory, the South suffered a serious accident. Late evening on May 2, a North Carolina regiment saw what it thought was Yankee cavalry and fired effectively. The men on horseback proved to be General Jackson and his staff on a reconnaissance mission. Jackson was struck fatally, and Lee lost his most effective weapon.

THE DARING PLAN TO TAKE VICKSBURG

Back in the west, Grant had now deliberately placed himself in the middle of the enemy, and although his engineers had opened up a water-line for his barges carrying supplies from Milliken's Bend to New Carthage, his long line of supply, since it now curved around the enemy's flank, was very exposed. But his resolute purpose outweighed textbook strategy. Having crossed the Mississippi, he collected wheeled transport for five days' rations, and leaving Sherman behind in charge, he cut loose from his base altogether on May 7th.

Virgil to Eliza

Dear Eliza

I write you a few lines to let you know where I am. This place is about 28 miles from Vicksburg towards Port Gibson. We came here Wednesday night and are now acting as sort of body guard to General McClernand, a very nice position.

I presume that long before you receive this you will have heard of the battle near Port Gibson on the first day of May - the battle we-call of Magnolia Church we call it - as it was near a church of that name. We left the river about 12 Thursday night travelling all night a distance of about 14 miles arriving on the ground field about 9 A.M. The fight had been begun by the rebs on our advance about daylight. Soon as we got on the ground the boys dropped their knapsacks, & immediately we took our position. The ground was very broken & hilly, hills covered with cane & almost impassable. We were engaged more or less during the entire day. The battle lasting until dark, when the rebels

114

gave way & retreated and we bivouaced for the night glad of a little rest, having in the moving double quicken for 3 miles & had nothing to eat all day. Not even time in the morning to make coffee. Consequently we were very tired & hungry. Our regiment escaped without losing a man. Not one wounded even seriously.

Our Army suffered but little 500 will a great deal more than cover our loss in killed & wounded. The rebels loss was severe, a great many killed, among them one General. We also took at least 1000 prisoners. They took none from us of consequence.

In the morning - Saturday - we marched into Port Gibson, the rebs having burned the bridge the pursuit was delayed a while, but we soon built a new bridge & were after them. They are now all over Black River & near Vicksburg & are preparing to cross. We may have a fight at Vicksburg but many think not, but if we do success is certain, our force being sufficient for any emergency. Vicksburg must come down now. I think they will evacuate & leave it to us. You must not be uneasy. All will be well & we will be safe. I would have written before this but have had no chance to send & don't know when this will go.

The 68th are here all well. Whit is in good health. They did not get into the battle. They did not arrive until it was over.

Our boys are all well, & in fine spirits expecting soon to be in Vicksburg

You may look for me home soon after Vicksburg is taken. An order has been issued from the War Department dismissing certain officers where the regiment has been reduced below 500 men. The companies are to be consolidated, & all supernumerary officers mustered out. The Col. & Major & all company officers over a sufficient number to officer the reduced number will go home. I think it a good move & will be a great saving to the government which is needed just now.

You will arrange your business matters accordingly, leaving all for me to attend to, except such as is absolutely necessary for your present necessities.

You need not say much about this matter as all will see me when I come. No letters from you but the one of April 9.

Good bye for the present
V. H. M.

THE INVESTMENT OF VICKSBURG

Virgil was wrong again. All didn't prove to be well, and Virgil's homecoming was nothing like the one he imagined and wrote about.

Now free to move, Grant moved north from the Big Black River, so as to interpose his army between the Confederate forces at Vicksburg where Pemberton had 30,000 men and those at Jackson, Mississippi where Johnston had another 25,000. By this time reinforcements for Grant's army had brought his strength from the 33,000 that he had originally brought across the river to a numerically superior force of 75,000.

A fight took place at Raymond on the 12th of May, and Jackson was occupied on May 14 just in time to prevent General Joseph E. Johnston from supplying reinforcements to Pemberton. Johnston, then supreme commander of the Confederates, ordered Pemberton to come out of Vicksburg and attack Grant. But Pemberton, who was being ordered by Jefferson Davis to hold Vicksburg at all costs, did not do so until he was too late.

117

On May 16th, when Pemberton did come out, Grant, with all his forces well in hand, defeated the Vicksburg contingent in the battle of Champion Hill, half way between Vicksburg and Jackson. On the following day Grant routed Pemberton's rear guard at the crossing of the Big Black River and drove the Confederates back into Vicksburg. Grant was finally able to occupy the high ground along the Yazoo which had been his objective from the beginning.

By May 18th Grant had his forces around Vicksburg so that it was cut off from external aid. He ordered a general assault at 2 p.m. on May 19th. The attack was made with great vigor but unsuccessfully, and the men were ordered back at nightfall. The next two days were spent in placing artillery and bringing up supplies to the troops and on the morning of May 22nd another general assault was made all along the line.

No men were visible in the hostile works except for a few sharpshooters, who were kept pretty quiet by the Union skirmishers. A volunteer storming party led Sherman's column. As they approached the works, they had to cross a bit of open ground in full view of the enemy. This they did on double quick and reached the salient of the bastion. As they approached the sally-port they were met by a withering fire. The front ranks wavered. The rear pressed on valiantly, but it was impossible to face the storm of lead and iron, and they had to seek cover. But the head of the column scaled the outer face of the left face of the bastion, planted their colors, and then literally burrowed into the earth to gain shelter from the flank fire. However, the Confederate position proved too strong for this kind of assault.

VIRGIL

It was in this final assault on Vicksburg that Major Virgil H. Moats was wounded by a musket ball which shattered the tibia of his left leg and damaged the knee. He was removed from the field and was later transported to Memphis from which he was granted further leave on June 8th. Subsequently he was sent up river to Cincinnati. It was reported that army surgeons suggested that the wounded leg be removed, but Major Moats declined, as he was resolved to return home a whole man or not return at all. This was not an uncommon decision among soldiers during the Civil War. The hospitals and medical care were so bad that the sick and wounded often insisted on going into combat if they possibly could, preferring death from the enemy to death from medical quackery and incompetence.

The text of a bronze plaque on a monument at Vicksburg describes the action in which Virgil was mortally wounded.

Campaign, Siege, and Defense of Vicksburg,
1863
ASSAULT ON THE CONFEDERATE LINE OF
DEFENSE, MAY 22

The Union Army under the command of Maj. Gen. U. S.
Grant was composed of the 13th, 15th, and 17th Corps.
The Confederate Army, under the command of Lieut. Gen.
John C. Pemberton, was composed of Stevenson's, Forney's,
Smith's, and Bower's Divisions, and Waul's Texas Legion.
Bowen's Division and the Legion, in reserve, were engaged. The two armies were in position on their respective
lines as on May 19th, except that Waul's Texas Legion had
been assigned a position in rear of the left of Lee's
brigade on the left of Stevenson's Division. After a
heavy cannonade by every gun in position on the Union
line, assaults were made at 10 A.M.: by the 15th Corps at
the stockade redan on the Graveyard Road: by the 17th on
the right and left of the Jackson Road: and by the 13th
by the lunette on the Baldwin's Ferry Road, the railroad
redoubt, and the curtain between that redoubt and Fort
Carrott: Hall's Brigade of McArthur's Division, 17th
Corps. advanced close to the Confederate line on the
Warrington Road but did not assault: the colors of the
leading regiments were carried close to the Confederate
works at every point assaulted. A Brigade Headquarters
flag was placed on the parapet of the stockade redan.
Flags were placed on the parapet of the railroad.redoubt
and that work was temporarily occupied, but no permanent
lodgment was anywhere made. Assaults were made in the

121

afternoon: by the 17th Corps at the curtain between the railroad redoubt and the lunette on the Baldwin's Ferry Road. At that lunette, at the Jackson Road, and at the curtain north of Glass' Bayou: and by the 15th Corps at the curtain south of the Graveyard Road, at the stockade redan on that road, and at a point about one-third of a mile west of that redan: the colors of the leading regiments were again carried close to the Confederate line. Another flag was placed on the parapet of the stockage redan, but the effort to carry the Confederate line of defense by assault was unsuccessful at every point. Casualties: Union: killed 502, wounded 2550, missing 147, total 3199, sixty eight officers killed or mortally wounded. Confederate: Not fully reported.

John Richardson to Virgil

Camp neer Vicksburg Miss June 28 1863

Frend Verge

i have been waiting a long time to hear from you and yester day i heard that you had sent for E to meat you at cincinnatta so i thot you would get home by the time this letter got thar i have not heard one word how you got along but hope you ar better and your wound is almost well i am well at present excepting toothache and mi eye has been getting soar for the last two or three days and James Mesied has been pretty sick but is getting better the rest of the boys ar able to cum to the table last thursday logan bload one corner of that larg foart about three miles high and they had a pretty hard battle but did not gane much ground i guess whit has been over here 3 or 4 times and i was over thar once but i exspect he has writen al about it Sulavan returnd last wensday and mat has ben rite between his legs ever sence and he has told him that his papers has ben sent to columbus for by you for a commishion in our companey and he has appointed him 2 lieutenent and got col landrow to sign it exspecting that his commishion wil com along one of thees days

123

now if you ar able i wish you would try and
undo what you have don if you have anney
felings for the boys i think you will do it
if you want to save mi life as its for a
sertin as he puts on anney more stile around
me i shal knock him down and then i supoes i
wil get shot James elliet has commenst
growling agane about thoes smal debts that you
owe the boys if you wil send me a list of thar
names i wil pay them for i have got tiard of
hering it did you get a dollar o Partee on
the boat to buy confed money with

    wel good by write as sone as you can or
get sombodey to do it for you and let me know
how you ar getting along give mi love to the
fameley and oblige your frend

    John E Richardson to V. H. Moats

CHRONOLOGY 1863
July to December

BIOGRAPHY	HISTORY

JULY

Major Moats Dies

* Morgan's Raiders
*   Active
* Battle of
*   Gettysburg
* Vicksburg
*   Surrenders

AUG.
*

SEPT.
*

OCT.
*

NOV.

* Gettysburg
*   Address
* Battle of
*   Lookout Mountain

DEC.

* Lincoln declares
*   Amnesty

THE FALL OF VICKSBURG

Another assault was made on Vicksburg on the 25th of June. It was unsuccessful, but resistance was almost at an end. Grant thereupon decided to rely for a while on a siege operation. He set to work to entrench his men and these works were completed on July 3rd. Grant had been preparing to attack on July 6th. On the 4th of July the garrison at Vicksburg, 37,000 strong, surrendered.

Thus it was ended. This campaign had consumed one hundred and nine days. The Union army had captured 37,000 prisoners, including fifteen Generals; had driven before them and partially dispersed another large army under the ablest of rebel leaders; had captured Vicksburg, the Gibraltar of the South; had freed the Mississippi River from rebel control; and had split the Confederacy so that Texas, Arkansas and Louisiana were isolated from the other Rebel States.

THE BATTLE OF GETTYSBURG

Almost at the same time, the Battle of Gettysburg was occurring in the east. General George G. Meade, then in command of the Army of the Potomac, the fifth commander within less than a year, took up positions on Pipe Creek while Generals John Reynolds and John Buford were at Gettysburg. On the 1st of July the heads of Lee's columns engaged Buford's cavalry outposts, and the conflict began. All troops on both sides hurried to this unexpected battlefield.

After a great three-days' battle, the Army of the Potomac emerged at last with a decisive victory. The Union had lost 23,000 men and Lee had lost nearly one-third of his army. Both armies were so mauled in the engagement that neither was capable of further significant action for the remainder of the year. It rained hard at Gettysburg on July 4 and mercifully washed the blood from the grass.

While Gettysburg was a dramatic high point in the progress of the war and received most of the attention, partly because of

127

Lincoln's Gettysburg address the following November, of the two events on July 4, 1863, Vicksburg was undoubtedly more important than Gettysburg for its effects on the course of the war.

VIRGIL

Major Virgil H. Moats died of his wounds received at Vicksburg. He had managed to reach Memphis and then travel by boat to Cincinnati on his way to his home in Defiance County, Ohio but he succumbed in General Hospital in Cincinnati on July 11.

Eliza traveled by train to Cincinnati to meet her hero husband accompanied by one of the sons. One account says that it was Douglas who was then less than four years old.

Along with the grief such an occasion would engender, the trip must have been frightening as well. It was at that time that Morgan's Raiders were carrying on their spectacular but futile raids in Kentucky, Indiana and Ohio. Morgan was attempting to reach Lake Erie where he had boasted that he would water his horses. The Raiders tried to follow and capture the train bearing Virgil's body, but they were unable to board it. They did, however, tear up the tracks behind it. As a result, Virgil's sister, Aunt Lydia Medkirk of Cincinnati, who had planned to come for the funeral the following day, was unable to attend.

Virgil's grave at Brunersburg, Ohio is marked by a tall and elaborate stone. Unfortunately, a soft sandstone was used. As a result a lengthy inscription on one side has been eroded by the weather and is no longer readable.

ROSECRANS TRAPPED IN CHATTANOOGA

In a series of successful maneuvers, General Rosecrans and his second in command, General Thomas, drove Bragg back into Chattanooga, Tennessee and then out of it. Later in defense of Chattanooga, in the battle of Chicamauga on September 19-20 Rosecrans' Union forces suffered 16,600 casualties while successfully defending his position. Bragg's forces lost nearly 18,000. However, the remaining Confederates distributed themselves to leave Rosecrans trapped in Chattanooga with no access to the North and necessary supplies.

GRANT'S ARMIES DELIVER TENNESSEE

Grant was given supreme command in the west and had under him three armies. The Army of Tennessee was under Sherman, two corps from Virginia were hurried by rail to Tennessee to serve under Hooker, and what had been Rosecrans' Army of the Cumberland was now commanded by General Thomas. Hooker and his men from the Army of the Potomac fought and won the extraordinary "Battle above the Clouds" on Lookout Mountain and on September 25th, the Confederate center on Missionary Ridge was stormed by General Thomas and the Army of the Cumberland. Grant's triumph was decisive and with Burnside's earlier victory over James Longstreet at Knoxville, the struggle for Tennessee was over, the Confederacy had been driven out of of the state. Vicksburg, Gettysburg and Chattanooga were now in Union hands without serious threat of recapture by the South.

RELATIVE QUIET ON THE EASTERN FRONT

Nothing of real military importance was happening in the east in the latter half of 1863. The two armies, those of Meade and Lee took a long time to recover from the slaughter at Gettysburg. They spent the latter part of the summer and the fall in regrouping and staying out of serious trouble. There were feints, skirmishes and cavalry maneuvers, but neither General was anxious to do battle except under very favorable circumstances. Such conditions did not arise. On November 26-28, Lee did repulse an attempt by Meade to surprise him in the battle of Mine Run on the Rapidan River.

On December 8, 1863, Lincoln issued his Proclamation of Amnesty and Reconstruction in an attempt to ease the anxieties of Southerners concerning the consequences of giving up the fight.

1864

CHANGES IN COMMAND

After Chattanooga there were major changes in military command. On March 9th, 1864, Grant was made Lieutenant General and given command of all the Union armies. Bragg was relieved of command and replaced by General Joseph E. Johnston. Chattanooga became the Union base for invasion of the middle of the remaining Southern territories.

Sherman was given command of 100,000 men in the west. Under him he had General James B. McPherson at the head of the Army of the Tennessee, General George H. Thomas and his Army of the Cumberland, and General John M. Schofield with a small Army of the Ohio.

In the east Grant put General Henry W. Halleck in charge of the paper work in Washington, a job that he was thoroughly capable of carrying out. General George G. Meade was put in nominal charge of the Army of the Potomac, then about 120,000 men, but Grant also chose to stay in the field and Meade therefore had little of the freedom of action normal for a field commander. Grant also brought Philip H. Sheridan from the Army of the Cumberland to command the cavalry.

With the appointment of Grant there was also a major shift in strategy. Union forces had been scattered in a pattern of garrisons aimed at holding captured territory and further dissipated by minor operations. Now Grant chose to concentrate his men into two armies under himself and Sherman. These two armies assumed the task of destroying the remaining effective Confederate forces. It was Sherman's task to deal with the 60,000 man Army of Tennessee under General Joseph E. Johnson, and Grant's task to deal with the 60,000 man Army of Northern Virginia under General Robert E. Lee.

CHRONOLOGY 1864
January to June

BIOGRAPHY   HISTORY

JAN.
  *

FEB.
  *

MAR.
  *

APR.
  *

MAY
  * 1st Battle of the
  *   Wilderness
  * Sherman Begins Pur-
  *   suit of Johnston
JUNE
  * Stalemate at
  *   Petersburg
  * Johnston falls back
  *   on Atlanta

GRANT BEGINS HIS PURSUIT OF LEE

In early May, Grant moved into The Wilderness and Lee moved forward to meet him. On the 5th there began a two day battle in a bad place, and the Federal army was beaten with the loss of 17,500 men. Lee lost fewer than 8,000. Instead of retreating back to Washington which had been the previous pattern, Grant started moving his army south. When the men realized that they were not again retreating, cheers arose from the ranks. This pattern was to be repeated a number of times. This time the battle was simply moved to a new spot and went on continuously from the 8th of May to the 19th. At one point the Confederate lines were broken in an early morning surprise attack and the Federals captured thousands of men, two generals, and twenty guns. They were driven back in a counter attack and one of the bloodiest battles of the war followed. In the 'Bloody Angle' much of which was hand-to-hand combat, 12,000 men fell in one day in an area of one square mile.

Elsewhere Sheridan's cavalry made a thrust toward Richmond where he met Jeb

Stuart's cavalry at Yellow Tavern on May 12. In the ensuing fight, Sheridan was driven off, but Stuart was killed. In another action Federal General Franz Sigel fought a battle in the Shenandoah and was beaten at New Market. General Ben Butler, a political appointee who was militarily incompetent, advanced with a force up the James River and was beaten in a fight at Bermuda Hundred. He made camp there and was bottled up, awaiting rescue.

Grant continued to move to his south and to his left across rivers and creeks toward Cold Harbor Crossroads. An objective was to try to cut off the rail access to Richmond at Petersburg. Lee countered each move by interposing himself between Grant and Richmond. On June 3 Grant tried a frontal assault. It failed and the armies stayed in the trenches for ten days. At one point miners in the Federal Army dug a tunnel under the Confederate lines and planted a large charge of dynamite. When it was discharged, it blew a large hole in the Confederate lines, but General Burnside failed to take advantage of the opening. The Union had lost 60,000 men in the actions up to this point.

Lee sent Jubal Early with a force of 14,000 men through the Shenandoah to Silver Springs to threaten Washington. He hoped that Grant might be forced to withdraw at the insistence of Washington politicians. However, Grant sent sufficient forces to threaten Early who then had to return. The ploy had failed.

Grant broke contact and moved again toward Petersburg. William F. Smith with an advance group reached Petersburg which was held by Beauregard with only 2,200 men. Smith attacked and took part of the works, but stopped to await the arrival of more men. Even when they did arrive inexplicably he failed to move, and Lee had time to reinforce Beauregard. Siege was then the only possible remaining strategy against this stronghold.

At this point Grant had lost sixty percent of his original army. Lee had lost half of his general staff and his army was shrinking by the day. By the end of June Grant had succeeded in cutting one rail line into Richmond and had sent the cavalry to cut more. They succeeded in ripping up sixty miles of track, thus causing Lee great difficulty in supplying his remaining forces.

SHERMAN'S PURSUIT OF JOHNSTON

In the west the war consisted primarily in a drawn out campaign between General Sherman and General Johnston, followed by Sherman's famous or infamous march through Georgia to the sea. Operations began early in May, 1964, and five days of maneuvering and skirmishing around Resaca and Rocky Face ended in Johnston retiring on Resaca. Johnston was unwilling to fight until he could maneuver himself into a favorable position for combat. A fortnight later, using essentially the same maneuvers against the Confederate defenses, Sherman caused Johnston to fall back again. At Adairsville the same process was gone through, and Johnston retired to Cassville, where he offered battle.

Sherman was as wary as Johnston and refused to be drawn into action under unfavorable circumstances. If each general had been able to obtain a great battle under his own terms, each would have fought most willingly, for neither desired a useless prolongation of the war. As it was, both declined to risk a decision.

As Johnston retreated southward, Sherman had to detach more and more men to maintain his communications back to Chattanooga. As a result, the Union superiority in numbers slowly decreased. Heavy combat did occur at Pickett's Mills and New Hope Church, May 25-27. Johnston gradually fell back and on the 6th of June, Federals appeared before Marietta. Heretofore, neither leader had offered a weak spot to his opponent, although Sherman had lost about 9000 men and Johnston about 6000 in the constant skirmishing.

Both Sherman and Johnston were concerned with the growing feeling that the skirmishing and maneuvering represented fear. Partly to dispel this perception, Sherman attacked Confederate entrenchments resulting in heavy fighting, notably at Pine Mountain on June 14th and at Kennesaw on the 27th. Subsequently the previous tactics were resumed.

As Sherman moved south toward Atlanta, his supply lines grew lengthy and vulnerable to attack by Bedford Forest and his effective cavalry. Early in June Sherman sent Major General Samuel D. Sturgis into central Mississippi to deal with Forest. When contact was made, Sturgis was thoroughly beaten in spite of a two to one advantage in numbers.

In a second maneuver Sherman sent Major A. J. Smith out of Memphis to attack Forest. This attack also failed to destroy the Rebel force. However, Forest was wounded and conducted subsequent maneuvers from a buggy with his wounded leg propped up before him. While the Confederates could be said to have won these military engagements, the primary effect was to keep Forest occupied in Mississippi and therefore keep him from harrassing Sherman's lines of supply out of Tennessee.

In time Johnston evacuated the Marietta lines, and on the 7th of July his fortifications on the Chattahoochee were turned and he fell back on Atlanta.

Johnston was replaced by General J. B. Hood who was given command with the understanding that he would 'fight.' He promptly did so. At first the Confederates were successful, but in the end they had to retire. A few days after this battle, called Peach Tree Creek, the battle of Atlanta took place. Even though the Union General McPherson was killed in this engagement, Hood again was beaten. The Army of the Tennessee under its new commander, General O. O. Howard, fought and won the critical battle of Ezra Church on July 27th, ending Confederate defense of Atlanta.

CHRONOLOGY 1864
July to December

BIOGRAPHY   HISTORY

JULY
* Battle of Ezra
* Church

AUG.

LWR to Eliza   * Farragut Enters
near Atlanta   * Mobile Bay

SEPT.
* Atlanta Falls

OCT.
* War Ends in Far
* West
* Sheridan Defeats
* Early

NOV.
* Lincoln
* Reelected
* Sherman Begins
* March to Sea

DEC.
* Fall of
* Savannah
* Thomas Defeats Hood
* in Tennessee

FARRAGUT AT MOBILE BAY

On August 5, Farragut drove his ships into Mobile Bay past the forts protecting the entrance. There he engaged and finally took the Confederate ironclad Tennessee. The harbor was heavily mined, and mines of this kind were then called torpedoes. It was when one of the smaller boats of Farragut's fleet hit a mine and was severely damaged that Farragut issued his famous order, "Damn the torpedoes - full speed ahead."

THE FALL OF ATLANTA

With Atlanta nearly surrounded, Hood was forced to adopt the previous tactics of maneuvering and skirmishing and left Atlanta to the Federals. An attack on the Army of the Ohio near Jonesboro concluded the Atlanta campaign. Atlanta fell on September 2nd.

Wages of War

L. W. Richardson to Eliza.

Camp 68th Regt OVI
Near Atlanta Ga.
August 4th 1864

My Dear Sister

        Your welcome letter bearing date July
10th but post marked 20th came Safe to hands
on the 26th I was glad to hear from you and
to learn you were all Enjoying So good Health
and were getting allong So well your letter
found me in very good health but prety well
worn out by constant fatieuge Knight watching
Fighting &c as we had just passed through a
Severe Battle in which our Corps Divis Brigade
and Regt were all Engaged with considerable
loss and it was a Severe contest as the Enimy
made a desperate Effort to turn and cut off
the left wing of our Army from the right which
consisted of our 17th Corps under Blair and
the 16th under Gen Dodge. the one had got
within 1½ miles of the City of Atlanta and in
Some places our line was not over 3/4 of a
mile from the out Skirts of the City. the
Rebs had laid a Trap to take us in by letting
us come up that close with litle Resistance,
dureing the Knight of the 21st they massed
nearly all their force on our left and on the

149

22nd about 11 P.M. they came down on our left flank in full force Expecting to crush us cut us off from the rest of the Army Capture our Train and Take us prisoners or drive us into the Chatahousee River they made a desperate charge and did take us a litle by Surprise at first but our men met them and Stood their ground and fought like Tigers which Saved our Army from a Severe Repulse the Enimy were completely failed in their object and were forced to Retreat with very Heavy Loss 3 times as much as ours they left the most of their dead & wounded on the Field in front of our lines it was a hard Sight the next day to witness. Our Regt lost about 65 in all killed wounded & missing My Co lost 2 killed & 8 wounded the Capt was Shlightly Scratched and left the field and the Co with me as I was the only Comsd officer left with them and have been since and it has confined me very close the Capt is more able for duty now and has been all that time than I am the Col says he shal come to the Co and I guess he will now. this Campaign has been a very hard one and we all feel prety well worn out We have the City of Altanta prety well Surrounded now and have had Several prety hard fights lately and have come out victorious Everytime and I think the Enimy has prety much concluded they can not drive us back as they they have tried it very hard all most every day for the last week and have been badly whiped every time we keep closeing in around them more and more every day I think the object is to capture their main force if possible and So end the war in in this department as I think we could take Atlanta now any day. well now I Shal have to close our Corps now occupy the Centre and are about 2 miles from the City it has been very qiet with us for several days and we have had a prety good chance to rest which we could appreciate if we remain where we now are on the line I dont think we will have much to do as the fighting I think will mostly be done on the Right and left I got a letter from Boyd dated 16th July was qite well I also get letters from home qite often You and E must write oftner to Me.

ps Direct Lieut L.W.R.
Co G. 68th OVI
2d Brigade
3 divis
17 a c
Atlanta, Ga.

THE END OF THE WAR IN THE FAR WEST

In the Fall of 1864 Sterling Price with a force of 12,000 Confederate soldiers rode into Missouri, On October 23 he was met by Samuel Curtis, who had been the victor at Pea Ridge. A battle occurred at Westport, Missouri and Price's men were defeated and driven into Arkansas. This action ended the war in this area.

ACTION IN THE SHENANDOAH VALLEY

While Grant and Meade kept Lee occupied, Sheridan was ordered to defeat Jubal Early and to waste the Shenandoah Valley to deny Lee this source of food. Sheridan met Early at Winchester on September 19 and drove Early before him. Again on September 22 Sheridan attacked Early at Fisher's Hill and beat him again. On October 19th Early attacked Sheridan, but in a counter-attack, Early's remaining forces were so damaged that this Confederate group was reduced to impotence.

THE PRESIDENTIAL ELECTION

The Democratic party had nominated General McClelland as its candidate for the presidency. A major element of the campaign was a desire on the part of many Northerners to end the bloody war and permit the South to go its own way. To some it did not seem to offer any real prospect of success. Many historians feel that the outcome of the election that November was determined on the battle field. Sherman's capture of Atlanta, Farragut's taking of Mobile, with Sheridan's successes in the Shenandoah Valley provided the stimulus to rearouse hope for a successful conclusion in favor of the Federal Army.

In November Lincoln was elected for a second term. He drew 2,203,831 votes to 1,797,019 for McClelland. Confidence had been restored.

SHERMAN'S MARCH TO THE SEA

Bedford Forest was again in action and was causing disturbances in Tennessee. Sherman made two decisions. He sent General Thomas north to deal with Forest and to restore order in the area. Simultaneously he decided on a radical change in tactics. Instead of further pursuit of what was left of the Confederate Army under Hood, he decided to ignore him. Instead of remaining attached to the supply lines back up into Tennessee, he chose to live off the land. On November 15 he started his march to the sea. For over a month few in the North knew where he was or what he was doing. With three armies moving in parallel he crossed Georgia foraging from the inhabitants and wasting much of what he could not use. Savannah was taken on December 20.

With Sherman out of the way, Hood started north in pursuit of Thomas. When Hood and Forest managed to join, the Confederates had about 30,000 men against the 40,000 Thomas commanded. Hood overtook a part of Thomas' army under Schofield at Franklin. In the battle there he lost 6,252 of the 18,000 men he had sent in the fray. He also lost seven generals. Six were killed and one was captured. The Union losses were 2,326.

Hood reached Nashville with 23,053 men against the 55,000 Thomas had now assembled under his command. On December 15th and 16th Thomas struck Hood and drove him south. Forest fought a rear guard action with 5,000 men and in so doing permitted Hood to escape across the Tennessee. However, Hood was relieved of his command and the few soldiers who were left were reassigned elsewhere.

1865

CHRONOLOGY 1865
January to June

BIOGRAPHY		HISTORY
	JAN.	
LWR to Eliza	*	
Near Vicksburg	*	
	FEB.	
	*	Sherman Starts
	*	North
	MAR.	
	*	Lee Attack Fails
	APR.	
	*	Sherman Takes
	*	Five Forks
	*	Grant Breaks
	*	Lee's Lines
	*	Lee Surrenders
	*	LINCOLN
	*	ASSASSINATED
	MAY	
	*	
	JUNE	
	*	

L. W. Richardson to Eliza

Camp   68th Regt   OVI
Near Vicksburg Miss   Jan 8th 1865

Dear Sister Eliza

    Your Welcome letter bearing date Dec 6th
& 13th came Safe to hand and was Thankfully
Received and Read with much Satisfaction and
Interest I was glad to hear that you were all
as well as usual and were getting along So
well I had heard from you by the way of home
a few days before I Received your letter As I
got qite a long letter from Ellen Stating that
Frank was out there on a visit and that the
Boys and children generally were having a good
time.

    Your letter finds me in very good health
which I have Enjoyed Since I last Saw you I
have got along first Rate as we have been
Stationed here Ever Since I Returned as we
were before I left. Since last July - and as
matters now Stand I Expect to come home as
will the Majority or over 3/4 of the Regt.
Before going anywhere Else. I am in hopes to
See you all if nothing hapens unusual. before
two months Roles around, as over the 3/4 of
the Regt has Reinlisted as vetrans and are to

come home as a Regt all and have a Furlough of 30 days in our own State and at <u>home</u> after which we are to Reorganise and Return to the Field again we may not leave the State for 2 months after we get home. officers can Serve their time out and then do as they chose about Reinlisting, 3/4 of the Co to which I belong has Reinlisted and I Expect to go home with them to pioneer ~~wherethe~~ which is in the vicinity of where the most of it was Raised

I was glad to hear you had Such good luck in Selling off your old Trumpery and Stock &c. I think you got good prices on an avrage and done well in getting the things and Stock off your hands when you did

I hope you and the children will Keep well and I think you will get along first Rate ~~you~~ I was glad also to hear you Say that you did not mean to let your Business worry you, and that you were like to meet all your Engagements and get your maters fixed up to Suit you. I know you can as no one can take any advantage of you at present Even were they So disposed. So I don't want you to Worry about anything in that line or anything Else as it will make it no better. I have two or 3 letters from John Since he went down the River from here and have writen him Several times the last one I got from him about a month ago contained good news for us all. he had seen Bro George and talked with him Said he was

161

Well and had Just Returned from Some great
Expedition in Banks Department Back to New
Iberia not far from Neworleans and thats about
all he wrote about him I Sent the Johns letter
to our folks at home as I Knew they would be
very anxious to Know Just what John Said about
him he Said he had grown So large he did not
Know him at first when he Saw him I am in
hopes to hear from him in person as I have
writen two letters to him Since I got Johns
letter I cant See why he has not writen to
any of us. I am glad to hear the Boys do So
well. I knew frank would be a good Steady Boy
and I guess Bill will come out all Right Dud
and Charley I cant tell what Sort of chaps
they will be yet. I guess they have a pretty
good large amount of their Mothers Spunk in
them, and may Reqire Some Sprouting, as She
used to, but Should they have as good a
faculty to get along without it and have the
Inocent chastised as it used to be the fate of
their abused Unkle then it is hard to tell
what the Result will be, but we must hope Such
will not be the case and that they will be
well Raised and make Excellent young men like
their Unkle tell Will and Frank that when I
get home I want them to go out hunting with
me. we will have Some tall times.

it may be I will have time to Break Orley to
Ride and drive and we can all go out to
Fathers in pioneer to geather I Send My best
Respects to Mr Smith and Family also to Mr.

Mocks folks. I hope the old women and girls and coperheads have Declared peace on Mud Creek Since Election is over I Suppose not there are but very few now who will own they Ever voted for or Supported him. he as well as all copperheads are dead and Burried and what are not will be Burried when the Soldiers all come home if they cherp a word of Treason or Speak disrespectful of us or the cause for which we are fighting "thats whats the mater (thats all on politicks)

I hope this will find you all well and that I may Soon be permited to See you all in person and face to face Soon So I will now close with best Respects to you and Frank Will & Dud Charlie and the dogs and

From your Bro

L. W. Richardson
p.s. Enclosed I send a black picture for Bill
L.W.R.

The 'pioneer' in this letter is a reference to Pioneer, Ohio, north of Defiance.

'Bro. George' is Eliza's brother George Newton Richardson, 24 years old at this time.

CONVERGENCE ON RICHMOND

On February 1st Sherman started north from Savannah with 60,000 veteran soldiers. Schofield with 21,000 joined him in North Carolina. The Confederates had assembled a rag-tag army of 30,000 men under Johnston to oppose Sherman.

On March 25th Lee launched an attack on the center of the Federal line in an effort to cut the railroads and thus the lines of supply for Grant's forces. The slim hope was that such an attack, if successful, would induce Grant to move his army back to Washington. If that occurred, Lee would have been able to move south and join Johnston. Unfortunately this last-gasp attack failed, and Lee had no other option than to retire back into the Confederate lines before Richmond.

On April 1st Sheridan with 12,000 men moved to occupy Five Forks to cut the rail lines and interpose himself between Lee and Johnston. He was opposed by men under George Pickett. Sheridan shattered the Confederates. He took 5,000 prisoners, and the survivors fled out of military control. No vestage of this Southern army remained. Sheridan was now firmly in place between Lee and Johnston.

On April 2nd Grant finally broke the center of the Confederate line at Petersburg. Lee evacuated that evening, and at the same time the government and the few military units that remained there fled Richmond.

Lee put what remained of his army on the road in a forced march in an effort to reach and join with Johnston. Sheridan forced this movement to drift to the west. On April 9th at Sayler's Creek the Federal cavalry and infantry struck Lee's rear, destroyed his wagon train and took thousands of prisoners. Lee now had fewer than 30,000 men, his supplies were destroyed, and there was little hope of replacing them. There were no means of further resistance.

Lee surrendered at Appomattox Court House on April 9th bringing military hostilities to a close. Five days later, on April 14th, Lincoln was assassinated at Ford's Theater in Washington. He died on April 15th. The Proclamation of General Amnesty issued on May 29th brought the futile, bloody war to a close.

POSTSCRIPTS

ELIZA

Readers may wonder about the fate of Eliza and the four sons of Virgil. She remained a widow for fifty years and raised the boys to manhood and independence as farmers. It might be supposed that one of the most important events in a farming community where land is of the essence was that Eliza ended up with the farm. The records do show that for $2,834.80 she obtained sole title from the four sons in a settlement of Virgil's estate twelve years after his death. This result is attested to in the following document.

3391

John B. (Hooliman)   Sheriff,

TO

Eliza Moats

Sheriff's Deed

Received July 10   1875

Recorded August 30"   1875

In   Defiance   County

Records Vol. 23,   Pages 544, 45 & 46

Lewis (Grill)   Recorder

Entered for Transfer

(Seal: "Transferred, Defiance Co. Ohio
John H. Conkle, Auditor.
Jul 10, 1875)

170

Sheriff's Deed

To All People to whom thse Presents shall come - Greeting:

Know Ye, That whereas, heretofore, to-wit: At the September Term, A. D. 1874, of the Court of Common Pleas of the County of Defiance and State of Ohio Eliza Moats administratrix of the estate of Virgil H. Moats, deceased in a certain Civil Action pending in the Court of Common Pleas, aforesaid, wherein Eliza Moats administratrix of the estate of Virgil H. Moats deceased, Plaintiff, and Frank W. Moats, William F. Moats, Charles V. Moats, & Douglass B. Moats, Defendants, for the sum of twenty-eight hundred and thirty-four dollars and eighty cents:

And Whereas, on the seventh day of November A. D. 1874 a certain order of sale was duly issued by said Court, directed to John B. Hooliman Sheriff of Defiance County and State of Ohio, commanding said Sheriff to proceed according to law and appraise, advertise and sell the lands and tenements hereafter described according to the statute in such cases made and provided:

And Whereas, having caused said Real Estate to be duly appraised, and a copy of the appraisement to be duly filed in the office of the Clerk of said Court, and having first given at least thirty days previous notice of the time and place of sale thereof by causing the same to be published five consecutive weeks in the Defiance Democrat a paper printed in and of general circulation in said County of Defiance; And Whereas, on the 19 day of December A. D. 1874 the said John B. Hooliman Sheriff exposed the said Real Estate for sale at Public Auction at the door of the Court House in said County of Defiance Ohio and the same was then and there sold to Eliza Moats for the sum of twenty-six hundred and thirty-six dollars and -------------- cents, being the highest bidder thereof, and said sum being more than two-thirds the appraised value thereof:

And Whereas, at the January Term of said Court, A. D. 1875, the said proceedings, by the said Sheriff had in the premises, were submitted to said Court and by it in all respects confirmed, and said Sheriff was ordered and directed to make a DEED of said Real Estate to said Eliza Moats

Now Know Ye, That I, John B. Hooliman Sheriff of Defiance County, Ohio by virtue of the Statute in such case made and provided, and in consideration of the sum of $2636 dollars and ----- cents to me in hand paid, the receipt whereof is hereby acknowledged, have Given, Granted, Bargained and Sold, and by said presents do hereby Sell and Convey unto the said Eliza Moats, heirs and assigns forever, the following lands and tenements situated in the County of Defiance and State of Ohio, and described as follows, to wit:

the North West quarter of the North East quarter of Section nine (9) and the West half of the North East fractional quarter of Section four (4) containing 78 acres also the West part of the East half of the South East quarter of Section four (4) containing 20 acres all in the township number four (4) North of Range three (3) east in Defiance County Ohio

To Have and Hold, the same with all the appurtenances thereunto belonging to her and her heirs forever,

In Witness Whereof, I have hereunto set my hand and seal officially this 7th day of May A. D. 1875   John B. Hooliman, Sheriff of Defiance County
Signed, Sealed, and Delivered in the Presence of S. T. Sutphen   Edwin Phelps

On this 7 day of May A. D. 1875, personally came before me, the undersigned Clerk of the Court in and for said County John B. Hooliman Sheriff of said Defiance County, Ohio, and acknowledged that he did voluntarily sign, seal and deliver the above Deed, for the uses and purposes therein expressed. Given under my hand and official seal of office the day and year last above written.

Edwin Phelps Clerke
Defiance County Common Pleas

Seal of the Common Pleas Court of the County of Defiance.

(Note: Material written in pen and ink is underlined.)

THE 48TH OHIO VOLUNTEER INFANTRY

Virgil's Regiment, The 48th Ohio Volunteer Infantry, continued in sporadic fighting, suffering further attrition in battles at Jackson and Bayou Teche. Then at Sabine Cross Roads in Louisiana, after giving a good account of itself, it was overrun and captured on April 8, 1864. It has been related that the colors of the regiment fell during this action, but was picked up by one of the older men who detached it from its staff and stuffed it into his haversack. When the men reached Camp Ford, Texas where they were imprisoned, it was given to Captain Gunsaullus who sewed it inside his blouse.

They were finally exchanged at the mouth of the Red River on the Mississippi on October 28, 1864. When they were finally aboard a Union boat, the flag was again raised. After the exchange, the regiment participated in the capture of Mobile and the remaining 105 men were then ordered to Texas. The 48th OVI was consolidated with the 83rd regular infantry on January 17, 1865, and were finally mustered out of the service at Columbus, Ohio on May 21, 1866.

The roster of Company F as printed in the HISTORY OF DEFIANCE COUNTY is:

Virgil H. Moats, Captain, promoted Major, died at Cincinnati from wounds received at Vicksburg; Aquilla Conrad, First Lientenant; Daniel Gunsaullus, Second Lieutenant; William H. Smith, First Sergeant, promoted First Lientenant; Frederick W. Hoeltzel, Second Sergeant; Homer W. Moats, Third Sergeant, died 1862; John Rath, Fourth Sergeant, died at Defiance on his way home, December, 1864; George W. Laser, Fifth Sergeant; Edward J. Todd, Wagoner; William H. Doud, First Corporal; John E. Richardson, Second Corporal; James Elliott, Third Corporal; Demetrius L. Bell, Fourth Corporal; Robert Cosgrave, Fifth Corporal; Frederick Speaker, Sixth Corporal; Philip Roberts, Seventh Corporal; Charles Marfilius, Eighth Corporal; William W. Russell and George A Williams, Musicians.

Privates: J. Arnst; H. Arnold, Metcalf A. Bell; Charles Bamler; E. Byers; George Byers; Charles Burger; George Blair; Eugene Brant; D. M. Bell; Thomas Brannan; John Butler; F. G. Bridenbaugh; William J. Cole; William E. Carpenter; Cornelius Conard; Edwin Cary; Michael Charl, enlisted 1864; Michael Carroll; William Donley; Edward Doud; William Ellis; Mathew Elliott; William Edwards; Lewis Ferris; Benjamin Gripps; Nelson D. Grogg; George G. Hopkins; David

Hollinbaugh; Daniel Hannah; Frederick Helmick; Harman Hockman; Frederick Hoeltzel; John M. Johnson; G. W. Janes; Paul Jones; John J. Kane, killed at Vicksburg, May, 1863; Joseph Kibble; Robert Kibble, died at Shiloh, March, 1863; Samuel Kochel; Isaac E. Kintigh; Patrick Kearney; John Kead; C. Lowry; William Lawrence; James Lawrence; Emanuel Miller; F. R. Miller; Philip Miller; George Morrison; James Myers, died in hospital November, 1863; George Minsel; James McFeeters; Philip McGuire; Joseph McKillips; Charles McHugh; Edward McVickers; H. Nolan; Christopher Nagle; Thomas O'Rourk; John E. Partee; Joseph Partee; Obadiah W. Partee; Dennis L. Pitts; Isaac Randall, died of disease at Bolivar, Tenn., August 6, 1862; Emanuel Reisch; John Rhinehart; Elias Ridenour; Isaac Ridenour; Rudy Rider; S. F. Roush, died at Shiloh, March 26, 1862; Rhoda Ryan; James Sanders, died in hospital at Albany, 1862; Robert Sanders; Andrew Schmidt; Matthias Shellinberger; Wentlin Shiels; Andrew Smith; Francis M. Smith; Peter Smith, died in hospital at Shiloh, 1862; Jacob Snyder; Abraham Spitler; George Trostle, enlisted 1864; Jacob Taylor; Alvara Vanskiver, enlisted January 17, 1864; David E. Welker; A. W. Whipple; Charles E. Williams; Alfred Winters; William Wright.

VIRGIL H. MOATS BIOGRAPHY

Virgil H. Moats was born May 5, 1827, in Licking County, Ohio. One of his grandfathers was Henry Moats, an immigrant from Germany. Henry married Jane Jackson Moats who was a relative of President Andrew Jackson. The 'Father' in these letters was William Virgil Moats who was born in 1799 and died in 1881, having outlived his wife, Mary S., by eight years. William and Mary had six children. Virgil was the oldest followed by Homer who also died in the service of the Union Army during the Civil War. Other children were Edwin Bruce born in 1832, William Wallace born in 1840, and Lydia S. (Moats) Medkirk born in 1844. This sister is referred to in the letters as 'Aunt Lydia.' It was she who was prevented from attending Virgil's funeral by Morgan's Raiders. There was another sister, named Harriet.

Virgil, having moved to Defiance County, Ohio, married Sarah McKinney at Newark, Ohio. They had two children, Franklin Wallace, born September 22, 1850 and Rowena who died at 10 months of age. Sarah died May 13, 1854, and in June of 1855

Virgil married Eliza Richardson who had been born in St. Lawrence Co., N. Y., on February 6, 1833. The parents of Eliza Moats, John and Delia Richardson, were from Vermont. Eliza had a number of brothers and sisters. Among these were Lay Whitney Richardson, born in 1830, who wrote two of the letters in this volume and John Richardson, born in 1847, who was probably the author of the 'Frend Verge' letter. It is worthy of note that in 1863, when the fall of Vicksburg occurred, Lay Whitney was 34 years of age but John was only 16.

Eliza raised four children. Franklin Wallace was born in 1850, William Henry in 1856, Douglas, 'Dud,' in 1860, and Charles V. in 1861. Hattie died at the age of three years also in 1861. Thus, when Virgil entered the service, Eliza was left to manage the farm with four boys, the oldest of which was Frank, then eleven, and the youngest was Charles, an infant.

Virgil was educated in Licking County, now the site of Denison University. He was a school teacher and in 1849 quit teaching to farm in Delaware Twp., Defiance, Co., Ohio. He served four years as Justice of the Peace and two years as the Sheriff of Defiance County.

In 1847 Virgil enlisted in the cavalry at Newark as a corporal, and was mustered out in 1848.

When he entered in the 48th Ohio Volunteer Infantry, in 1861, he was described as being five feet, ten inches tall, of fair complexion with grey eyes and dark hair.

He enlisted October 13, 1861 and was appointed as a Second Lieutenant two days later. Less than a month later, on December 13, he was appointed Captain. He was appointed to the rank of Major in April, 1863 with rank and pay retroactive to February 21, 1863. Wounded on May 22, 1863 and died in Cincinnati on July 11.

INDEX

A

Adairsville, 143

Alton, Steamer, 43

Annapolis, 8

Antietam, 43, 50

Appomattox Courthouse, 165

Arkansas Post, x, 61, 87, 90, 93, 100

Arkansas River, 61, 90, 91, 93

Asboth, 71, 75

Atlanta, 139, 144, 145, 146, 148, 149, 150, 151, 154

B

Baily, Barbara, iii

Baltimore, 8

Banks, N. P., 106, 162

Baton Rouge, 106

Battle above the clouds, 132

Bayou Teche, 175

Beauregard, P. G. T., 7, 10, 22, 25, 29, 31, 33, 60, 142

Bermuda Hundred, 141

Beverly, 9

Bill, (See Moats), 101, 162

Black (Big) River, 115, 117, 118

Blair, 149

Blair, Geo., 93, 95

Bloody Angle, 140

Bowling Green, Kentucky, 22, 24

Boyd, 19, 151

Bragg, B., 31, 37, 55, 89, 131, 137

Brant, Eugene, 102

Brunersburg, Ohio, 46, 130

Brown, 44, 65

Brown, John, 7

Buell, D. C., 21, 29, 31, 32, 55

Buford, J. 127

Bull Run, First, 3, 10, 13

Burnside, A. E., 67, 68, 132, 141

Butler, 96, 141

C

187

188

O

R

S

194

W

Wagley, Phyllis, iii
Wal (Wall), 20, 34
Walker, Kathryn (Sage)
    iii
Wallace, L., 21, 24
Wallace, W. H. L., 30,
    31, 32
Washington, 8, 10, 12,
    48, 50, 51, 63,
    69, 88, 98, 112,

137, 140, 141,
    164, 165
Westport, 152
Whit, 19, 34, 39, 76,
    101, 116
White River, 91, 93
Wilderness, The, 139,
    140
Winchester, 153

Y

Yazoo River, 61, 73,
    77, 79, 83, 99,
    111, 118

Yellow Tavern, 141
Young's Point, 63

196